RICHARD HIMELFARB

CATASTROPHIC
POLITICS THE RISE
AND FALL
OF THE MEDICARE
CATASTROPHIC COVERAGE ACT
OF 1988

The Pennsylvania State University Press
University Park, Pennsylvania

Library of Congress Cataloging-in-Publication Data

Himelfarb, Richard, 1963–
    Catastrophic politics : the rise and fall of the Medicare
Catastrophic Coverage Act of 1988 / Richard Himelfarb.
        p.   cm.
    Includes bibliographical references and index.
    ISBN 0-271-01465-2 (cloth : acid-free paper)
    ISBN 0-271-01466-0 (paper)
    1. Medicare—Law and legislation.   2. Aged—Long-term care—Law
and legislation—United States.   3. Insurance, Catastrophic health—
Law and legislation—United States.   I. Title.
KF3608.A4H564   1995
344.73′0226—dc20
[347.304226]
                                                                95-4251
                                                                CIP

It is the policy of The Pennsylvania State University Press to use acid-free paper for
the first printing of all clothbound books. Publications on uncoated stock satisfy the
minimum requirements of American National Standard for Information Sciences—
Permanence of Paper for Printed Library Materials, ANSI Z39.48–1992.

CATASTROPHIC
POLITICS

Contents

List of Tables _____

Preface

In July 1988, congressmen and advocates for senior citizens heralded the enactment of the Medicare Catastrophic Coverage Act (MCCA) as the first major expansion of government health care for the nation's elderly since the creation of Medicare in 1965. The legislation effectively plugged many of the holes in the existing Medicare system by providing protection against a number of catastrophic health-care expenses, including those associated with acute hospital care, physician services, and prescription drugs. Support for the MCCA was virtually universal. The measure passed the House by a margin of more than 2 to 1 and the Senate passed it by almost 8 to 1; it was endorsed by President Ronald Reagan, by leading members of Congress, and by the 28-million-member American Association of Retired Persons (AARP); and public-opinion surveys indicated widespread and growing support for the MCCA among the nation's elderly. Backed by this apparent consensus, passage appeared to establish a precedent for expanding social-insurance programs in an era of high federal deficits. Indeed, some of the program's strongest advocates viewed the event as a precursor to the enactment of long-term care legislation in the near future.

Less than eighteen months later, the House and the Senate, responding to a torrent of criticism from the elderly, were voting by similar margins to repeal virtually all the legislation. At the same time, support within Congress for expanding Medicare to cover long-term care quickly evaporated. At least in the short run, the repeal had foreclosed the prospects for such a program.

How did such a remarkable turnabout occur, and why were MCCA supporters unable to foresee it? This study attempts both to answer these questions and to examine the larger implications of the episode. It argues that the key to understanding the passage and eventual repeal lies in the decision of Congress to depart from previous practice in the area of social-insurance policy-making. Specifically, in an attempt to expand Medicare in a deficit-neutral manner without imposing costs on younger generations, the new program imposed all costs on elderly beneficiaries themselves. In addition, costs were distributed in a progressive manner, in order to avoid burdening low-income senior citizens and to establish a precedent for future policy-making in social-insurance programs. With more than 60 percent of the elderly due to receive benefits from the program well in excess of its personal costs to them, MCCA architects envisioned widespread support for the program from most senior citizens.

Explaining the ensuing public outcry and the failure of MCCA architects to counter such criticism effectively is the central aim of this case study. More general issues, concerning the federal government's ability to expand programs for the elderly in an era of high deficits, and the nature of public opinion and its relationships to public policy, are addressed as well.

I have relied on a number of sources, primary among which are the interviews I conducted with principals and close observers of the MCCA representing both congressmen and interest groups. The interviews took place in Washington, D.C., between March 1990 and January 1992. Because none of the discussions was tape-recorded, the material mentioned here consists of reconstructed written notes taken during and immediately following the sessions. Because all subjects spoke on condition of anonymity, none has been quoted directly. Another source was survey microdata obtained from the American Association of Retired Persons (AARP), which provide the basis for the chapter discussing the dissatisfaction expressed by the elderly after passage. These data detail the trend of increasing senior-citizen opposition to the program and provide insights regarding its underlying causes. To examine how the legislation and subsequent repeal were portrayed to the public, I also reviewed videotape of approximately thirty-five stories appearing on the nightly network news between December 1986 and December 1989. The tapes were obtained from the Vanderbilt Television News Archives. I also rely on a considerable number of primary and secondary written resources. These include the significant public record of the MCCA contained in congressional hearings, government reports, and the *Congressional Record* as well as a number of unpublished documents obtained from congressional staff. In addition, journalistic accounts of the episode were studied extensively. Particularly useful was the reporting of the *New York Times,* the *Washington Post,* the *Wall Street Journal,* and the *Congressional Quarterly.* Invaluable as well was the AARP's monthly newsletter, the *AARP Bulletin.*

Chapter 1 outlines the public-policy context in which the MCCA was formulated. In Chapter 2 the evolution of the legislation is traced from the initial efforts of Otis Bowen to place the issue on the political agenda, through the "Christmas tree" expansion of the Bowen plan by Congress.

The political constraints and considerations that led the congressional architects of the MCCA to finance the legislation by imposing all costs on the elderly and by structuring premiums according to ability-to-pay principles are the topic of Chapter 3, which emphasizes the degree to which financing represented a departure from previous social-insurance policy-making. This chapter also explains the decision of the influential AARP to support (at least tacitly) the legislation's financing mechanism.

Chapter 4 focuses on the decisions of rank-and-file members of Congress to support MCCA. It begins with an analysis of the congressional debates over the legislation, paying particular attention to the degree of controversy surrounding financing. This is followed by a discussion of the influence of Claude Pepper, other political leaders, the AARP, and early public-opinion surveys (conducted by this organization) on rank-and-file congressional support for the legislation. Early media coverage of the program's development and passage is analyzed to explain the high degree of early public support for the program.

The rise of opposition to the MCCA on the part of the elderly in the months after passage is the topic of Chapter 5. The phenomenon of increasing opposition even among low-income elderly, virtually all of whom stood to receive significant benefits at little personal cost, is emphasized, and the degree to which this opposition resulted from misperceptions of the impact the legislation would have on them personally, particularly with respect to costs stemming from its supplemental premium, is examined.

Chapter 6 discusses the causes of increasing senior-citizen opposition to the MCCA, and the continuing confusion concerning its financing, which ultimately led to the repeal. Explanations emphasized include the program's failure to provide a comprehensive long-term-care benefit, in spite of being labeled "catastrophic coverage"; the role of the National Committee to Preserve Social Security and Medicare in misleading many of the elderly about the program's costs and encouraging grass-roots opposition; and, perhaps most important, the inability and failure of MCCA architects to explain clearly and frankly the redistributive implications of the program's financing. Also addressed is the failure of legislators to agree on an alternative that preserved more than a small fraction of the program's benefits.

Finally, Chapter 7 discusses the implications of the MCCA episode for future policy-making affecting the elderly.

To my parents

Acknowledgments ———————————————

While writing a book is a distinctly solitary experience, completing a project of such magnitude is impossible without the assistance of many people. My first set of debts lie with the numerous Washington professionals, congressional staffers, and interest group representatives alike, who through personal interviews (and in some cases written documents) provided me with significant insight into the episode under study. Only their desire for anonymity prevents me from naming them.

Major gratitude is also owed to the American Association of Retired Persons for permitting me access to the survey microdata analyzed in Chapter 5. Here a special thank-you to Margaret Straw is also in order, for she took time from her hectic schedule both to support my request and to prepare the material so it was easily accessible to a computer novice like myself. Appreciation is also extended to Jon Gabel and the Health Insurance Association of America for providing access to microdata from its own survey of public opinion concerning the Medicare Catastrophic Coverage Act of 1988.

At the University of Rochester, where this work originated, my thanks begin with some of the numerous graduate students I have been privileged to study with and know as friends. In particular, Melinda Cuddy, Rich Forgette, Roger James, Bill Kubik, Carol Silva, and especially Carolyn Whitfield deserve my gratitude for providing encouragement and support during this project. Wendy Schiller deserves special thanks for getting me a foot in the door with a number of influential staffers who may have been less open to speaking with me otherwise.

Members of the faculty at the University of Rochester deserve significant credit for the virtues of this study. Lynda Powell played a major role in the early stages of this project, among other things providing me with a crash course on SPSS-X that will serve me well beyond graduate school. Larry Rothenberg provided extensive advice and constructive criticism throughout my effort. He deserves profuse thanks both for his eagerness to help and for his abundant patience with the author.

Of course, my greatest debt of gratitude is owed to my adviser, Bruce Jacobs. Simply stated, this project would never have reached completion (or survived its infancy) without his steady guidance and incessant (although in hindsight perhaps necessary) cajoling. He continues to be my intellectual mentor. I hope that more than a few of the things he taught me are present in this study.

Here at Hofstra University, Paul Harper deserves special thanks for restructuring my teaching load so I could complete work on the manuscript.

A special word of thanks is also in order for Theodore Marmor, whose extensive and thoughtful critique of my work significantly improved the final product.

At Penn State Press, Sanford Thatcher, director, deserves credit for his eagerness to pursue this project and his assistance throughout the process. Peggy Hoover's expert copy-editing has smoothed over a number of rough edges and consequently made my work easier to read.

Finally, I must thank my parents, who always stood by ready to offer support, financial and otherwise, and my brother Saul, who procured a portable PC for me to use when visiting home. Last but by no means least, I thank Patricia Lee Stewart for extensive technical assistance with this manuscript and, even more important, the gift of her friendship during its completion.

1

SETTING THE STAGE FOR THE MEDICARE CATASTROPHIC COVERAGE ACT OF 1988

Among Western democracies, the United States is unique in its tendency to make the elderly the focus of public social-welfare programs. In the words of Theodore Marmor (1988, 178), "No other industrial democracy has compulsory health insurance for its elderly citizens alone, and none started its program with such a beneficiary group. Almost all other nations started with coverage of their work force, or, as in the case of Canada, went from special programs for the poor to universal programs for one service (hospitals) and then to another (physicians)." In contrast to other demographic groups in the population (for example, single mothers), Americans have historically viewed the elderly as a population deserving of public support. According to Marmor (1973, 16), Americans have subscribed to the belief that the elderly comprise "one of the few population groupings about whom one could not say the members should take care of their financial-medical programs by earning and saving more money."

This consensus has been further reinforced by the distinct design of the nation's Social Security system and the popular beliefs surrounding it. The fact that participation is virtually universal and that all participants are required to contribute something toward their retirement through payroll taxes[1] has conferred a degree of legitimacy and public acceptance on the system, absent in other social-welfare programs. Despite the significant redistribution occurring both between and within cohorts of participants,

---

1. According to Bernstein and Bernstein (1989, 14), Social Security in 1986 "covered 95 percent of the working population." The only significant groups remaining outside the system are "some public employees: the minority of employees of state and local governments that have not chosen such coverage and those employed by the federal government prior to 1984."

the public perceives all Social Security recipients as having "earned" their benefits through contributions to the system. This remains the case even though recipients have historically received benefits well in excess of the economic value of their contributions to the program (U.S. House, Committee on Ways and Means 1993, 1301–6).

Historically, advocates for the elderly and their political supporters have maintained a significant interest in perpetuating these beliefs by downplaying the degree of redistribution occurring within the system. To the extent that system participants are able to calculate exactly who gains more or less financially, Social Security could degenerate into a zero-sum game in which financial losers demand political redress or the opportunity to opt out of the system. Program advocates understand that voluntary participation would undermine one of Social Security's key goals, that of providing an adequate income to relatively poor elderly citizens through redistribution. If only low-income citizens were left to rely on Social Security, general revenues would probably be increasingly necessary to fund the program. Social Security advocates believe that such a program would pay smaller benefits to needy elderly as funding became dependent on the vicissitudes of federal budget-making. As Marmor, Mashaw, and Harvey (1990, 160) note, "No targeted welfare program, including those for the aged, provides anything approaching Social Security's benefit levels."

At the same time, because under a voluntary system participation would acquire a stigma similar to that occurring in federal public assistance programs (Bernstein and Bernstein 1989, 210–11), efforts to blur or hide the degree of redistribution in Social Security have preserved the program's antipoverty purpose.[2]

From the creation of Social Security through the mid-1970s, a number of factors combined to defuse potential conflicts concerning program goals. Part of the explanation has to do with the decision-making process surrounding the program itself. During most of Social Security's early history, "policy-making was undertaken by a relatively constricted and autonomous set of actors" within the Social Security Administration whose choices regarding the program "were generally made in isolation from decisions about other government activities" (Derthick 1979a, 7).

Other significant factors included (1) the decision to change Social

2. This impact is substantial. According to a calculation by the Congressional Budget Office, in 1991, social-insurance programs—the largest of which is Social Security—removed from poverty 72.9 percent of elderly Americans with pre-transfer incomes below the poverty line. See U.S. House, Committee on Ways and Means 1993, 1350.

Security from a fully funded system (where money held in trust funds is sufficient to pay all current and future benefit claims) to one utilizing the principle of pay-as-you-go; (2) periodic expansion of benefits and coverage to previously uncovered groups; and (3) economic growth. Together, these factors permitted the system to pay benefits to early cohorts of retirees well in excess of their contributions to the system without unduly burdening younger workers. Indeed, the "good deal" that older generations received throughout this period has probably increased support for the program among younger generations, even though most are not likely to receive similar returns when they retire.

As a result, the Social Security system has always been extremely popular among Americans of all ages. "In fact," report Page and Shapiro (1992, 119), "according to responses to some four dozen surveys by various organizations between 1961 and 1989, many more people always wanted to *increase* than wanted to decrease Social Security spending." At the same time, "very large majorities, on the order of 80–90 percent, have opposed cuts" in the program.[3] It is important to note that levels of support for Social Security among younger Americans have generally varied little from the support senior citizens have expressed. Indeed, one recent study of 1982 survey data reveals that the elderly were *less* likely than younger citizens to favor increases in program spending (Day 1990, 47).

Given the widespread public support for Social Security, it is not surprising that those seeking to design a health-care program for the elderly sought to do so within a social-insurance framework. However, because the structure of the Medicare program adopted in 1965 had "a political explanation, not a philosophical rationale" (Marmor 1988, 182), their efforts were only partially successful. On the one hand, Part A of the Medicare program, which covers hospital insurance, was structured similarly to Social Security, with universal participation and financing by younger cohorts through a payroll tax. Just as in Social Security, pay-as-you-go financing allowed early and, indeed, current beneficiaries to reap a considerable windfall from the program (in terms of the ratio of benefits to taxes paid [U.S. House, Committee on Ways and Means

3. Most such data probably represent "poor quality public opinion," because the survey questions on which they are based "fail to confront respondents with difficult trade-offs that directly challenge wishful thinking" (Yankelovich 1991, 42–43). For example, such items fail to ask how Social Security benefits are to be maintained or increased—through payroll-tax increases, benefit reductions, or some other method. Nevertheless, the consistency of such responses over time appears to demonstrate broad-based if somewhat vague public support for the program.

1993, 1301–4; Congressional Budget Office 1989; Vogel 1988]) while at the same time believing that they "earned" their benefits through payroll tax contributions. On the other hand, Part B (covering physician services) represented a departure from the intergenerational financing of Social Security and Medicare A. Under Part B, the elderly themselves paid a flat premium equivalent to 50 percent of physician costs (lowered to 25 percent in 1981), and general revenues from the federal government subsidized the remainder of the expenses.[4] Like these other programs, however, participation was a good deal for all beneficiaries because it provided coverage costing well in excess of recipients' actual contributions to the program. In addition, while the existence of subsidies in Medicare B was more apparent than in Social Security and Medicare A, most participants likely were unaware of their presence.

Two additional aspects of the early Medicare program also made it similar to Social Security at its beginning. First, there was the limited scope of Medicare benefits. While Medicare covered a portion of hospital and physician fees, significant deductibles and co-payments were included, in an effort to control program costs. Equally as important is that Medicare failed to provide any coverage in a number of areas, the most noteworthy being nursing-home stays and prescription-drug costs. Despite such limitations, a number of lawmakers predicted that the new program would expand incrementally to fill such gaps (Derthick 1979a, 334–35). Second, as with Social Security, Medicare's proponents "assumed that eligibility would be gradually expanded to take in most if not all of the population" (Marmor 1988, 179). In the case of Medicare, coverage would be extended "first, perhaps, to children and pregnant women."

By the late 1970s, however, a failing American economy and increasing inflation precipitated a significant retrenchment in federal programs affecting the elderly. In Social Security, inflation caused benefit payments to rise faster than expected, while unemployment caused revenues to decline relative to expectations. Observers predicted that, in the absence of reform, the Social Security retirement trust fund would be bankrupt by the mid-1980s. At the same time, the Medicare system, while not in immediate

4. The decision to finance Medicare B in this manner, instead of through payroll taxes, represented an intentional departure from a system relying solely on intergenerational financing. This change can be attributed to the desire of House Ways and Means Committee Chairman Wilbur Mills "to build a fence around the program" and "insure against later expansion of the social security program to include physician coverage" (Marmor 1973, 80). However, because 75 percent of Medicare B's cost is paid from general Treasury revenues, tax and fee payments from all age-groups (only a small percentage of which come from taxpayers age 65 and over) provide the bulk of funding for this program too.

danger, was faring even worse than Social Security as soaring health-care costs threatened to undermine the long-run integrity of the program.

The economic troubles of this period transformed the politics of federal programs serving the elderly. Whereas the 1960s and early 1970s had been marked by significant expansion of federal aid to the aged, the late 1970s and 1980s constituted an era of scarcity in which public officials struggled to maintain the gains of an earlier era. In short, from the Carter years onward, legislators would face no more "easy votes" on programs affecting the elderly (Derthick 1979b).

The Social Security Amendments of 1977 marked the first instance of policy-making in this new era. Intended to shore up the long-term solvency of the program through the year 2030, the legislation precipitously raised payroll taxes paid by workers in what at the time constituted the biggest peacetime tax increase in American history. Unfortunately, it became apparent almost immediately that the legislation would fall well short of expectations. By the early 1980s, increasing inflation and a stagnant economy were causing Social Security benefit payments to exceed contributions by $10 billion to $15 billion yearly. In the absence of further reforms, experts predicted the system would be bankrupt by as early as 1982.

President Ronald Reagan assumed office in 1981 with a mandate to reduce the size of government and cut taxes. In an attempt to confront Social Security's fiscal problems, as well as a growing deficit in the overall federal budget, Reagan set forth proposals to reduce benefits for early retirees and eliminate the program's minimum benefit. Both were quickly rejected and denounced, particularly by Democrats in Congress who accused Reagan of attempting to destroy Social Security and break the federal government's contract with the elderly. Indeed, the issue became a centerpiece in Democratic attacks on Reagan and the Republicans in the 1982 mid-term elections (Light 1985, 152–62).

Stung by public criticism of its proposals, the Reagan administration sought to distance itself from the Social Security issue, refusing to propose further reforms in the absence of Democratic cooperation. At the same time, however, the program's declining fiscal status required action. By late 1981, experts believed that the government had only months to avert bankruptcy in Social Security's retirement trust fund. These circumstances led Reagan to cede Social Security's problems to a bipartisan commission led by Alan Greenspan that would issue recommendations following the 1982 election.

A crisis atmosphere drove the deliberations of the Greenspan Commission. Indeed, the commission itself stoked this sense of urgency by voting to terminate interfund borrowing (by Social Security's retirement fund from its disability and Medicare funds) on the last day of 1982. This decision was intended as a prod both to commission members and to Congress generally. If the former failed to reach consensus or the latter failed to accept its recommendations, the consequences would range from merely embarrassing (the need to pass a quick-fix solution and revisit the issue shortly) to disastrous (benefit checks would likely stop in July 1983) (Light 1985, 136–37).

Working under enormous political pressure, the Greenspan Commission emerged with recommendations that ultimately proved acceptable to both Congress and President Reagan. The majority of reforms contained in the Social Security Amendments of 1983 continued in the mold of the 1977 legislation by imposing most of the bailout's costs on working-age adults. It is significant, however, that the legislation contained a pair of measures that for the first time explicitly affected benefits of current retirees—one freezing benefits for six months, the other providing for taxing half of Social Security benefits for single persons with incomes above $25,000 a year and for couples with incomes above $32,000. These measures were precedents in the history of Social Security policy-making. Never before had public officials enacted policies to reduce the real value of monthly benefits. More important, the introduction of explicit, visible income-relating within Social Security was particularly significant in light of ongoing efforts by advocates to avert such policies.

During the 1980s, the status of the Medicare system, though in the short-run less dire than that of Social Security, was even more worrisome. While Medicare faced a myriad of problems, the primary one concerned its cost, which rose sharply after its implementation in 1967, outpacing both the general cost of living and government revenues (Marmor 1988, 177). Between 1967 and 1985, spending on Medicare grew from $3.5 billion (2 percent of the federal budget) to $70 billion (over 7 percent). In the absence of reforms in program spending and financing, actuaries in 1985 projected that the Health Insurance trust fund (Part A of the program) would be insolvent by 1998 (Moon 1993, 61).

Medicare's financial problems stemmed from the design of the system, which had few controls on physician and hospital fees and provided many beneficiaries with little incentive to economize on the utilization of health care. During most of Medicare's early history, "the program paid hospitals 'reasonable costs' and physicians 'reasonable and customary fees' "

(Marmor 1993, 55–56). In effect, under this cost-based, retrospective payment system, "doctors and hospitals set their own incomes, courtesy of the U.S. treasury" (M. Peterson 1993, 796). At the same time, the program's failure to relate co-payments and deductibles to income, as well as the emergence of supplemental "Medigap" policies to cover such costs, led to major increases in the utilization of program benefits.

The first effort to rein in rising Medicare costs materialized in 1972 when the federal government established professional standards review organizations (PSROs) to review the care received by program beneficiaries. Ultimately, however, such bodies failed to restrain Medicare costs because they left intact the program's basic inflationary structure, particularly retrospective payment of physicians (Marmor 1988, 187).

By the 1980s, as the nation's health-care costs continued to spiral upward (exceeding even the substantial inflation rates recorded by the consumer price index), the Medicare program "acquired a greater salience" for policymakers (Marmor 1988, 193). Increasingly concerned with restraining the costs of public programs including Medicare's rapidly rising expenditures, Congress, prodded by the Reagan administration, undertook a series of piecemeal adjustments to the program. By the middle of the decade, payments to hospitals and physicians had been periodically frozen, a system of diagnosis-related groups (DRGs) was introduced to control costs, and increased cost-sharing had been imposed on Medicare and Medicaid recipients. These measures, however, were taken with little reevaluation of the basic policies guiding the system (Shick 1989). Beyond the budget implications for Medicare, their main effect was an implicit rationing of health-care benefits that occurred when access to health care decreased in response to declining reimbursements to hospitals and physicians. As this took place, the potential expansion of Medicare coverage to limit liability for acute hospital and physician costs, as well as to provide coverage for items such as prescription drugs and long-term care, was not seriously considered by public officials.

The Increasing Affluence and Political Power of Senior Citizens

Throughout this period, efforts to expand public programs for the elderly were also probably undermined by the growing affluence of senior citizens, both in terms of absolute standards of living and in relation to the rest of the population. Between 1970 and 1986, real median family incomes both of families headed by a senior citizen and of unrelated individuals who were elderly rose by 50 percent, a rate more than twice that of their nonelderly counterparts (Congressional Budget Office 1988a). During the same period, poverty among the elderly fell by almost half, from 24.6 percent to 12.4 percent. By contrast, poverty among persons aged 18 to 64 increased by 20 percent (from 9 percent to 10.8 percent) and among children by 26 percent (15.1 percent to 20.5 percent). Indeed, by 1982, the poverty rate for persons 65 and over fell below the rate for persons 64 and younger for the first time in American history (and has remained lower ever since) (Jacobs 1986a, 8).

Increasing well-being of senior citizens extended beyond income to assets. By 1984, Peterson and Howe (1988, 95) note, "56 percent of all elderly households had a net worth of at least $50,000; only 7 percent had a zero or negative worth. By contrast, only 23 percent of households headed by persons under 45 exceeded the $50,000 mark; and 15 percent had a zero or negative worth." The chief reason for this difference concerned home ownership. Almost three-quarters of elderly householders were homeowners, and 84 percent owned their homes free and clear (Jacobs 1986b). By contrast, among persons under 45 almost half were homeowners and nearly all had mortgages (Peterson and Howe 1988, 96).

In the 1980s, the increasing affluence of the nation's elderly was accompanied by their rise as a political force. "Senior power" manifested itself in two ways: at the ballot box and through elderly-based interest groups. The nation's growing elderly population was disproportionately represented among the electorate, in 1987 accounting for 12 percent of the population, but 16 to 18 percent of all voters in recent elections (Binstock 1987). Beginning in 1986, senior citizens voted in higher proportions than any other age-group (Stanley and Niemi 1992).

This phenomenon was accompanied by the growth and increasing visibility of senior-citizen interest groups seeking to exert influence on their behalf.[5] By 1988, the largest of these groups, the American Association of Retired Persons, boasted 28 million members and a yearly budget of $145 million. Approximately $10 million of this was devoted to the

5. The development of what Pratt (1976) called "the gray lobby" is a relatively recent phenomenon of the last two decades.

organization's legislative division, which employed a staff of 125, including 18 registered lobbyists (Tierney 1988). Although less prominent than the AARP, a number of other organizations also engaged in significant political activity on behalf of the political interests of senior citizens. These groups included the National Council of Senior Citizens, the National Committee to Preserve Social Security and Medicare, and Families U.S.A. (formerly the Villers Foundation).

Popular accounts have ascribed considerable political influence to the elderly and to the interest groups purporting to represent them (Hewlett 1991; Longman 1987; Peterson and Howe, 1988; Tierney 1988). Indeed, by the late 1980s they were frequently referred to as the "800 lb. gorilla of American politics," possessing considerable muscle and capable of overwhelming everything in its way.[6]

Undoubtedly, federal budget politics of the 1980s served to fuel such perceptions. During this period, the portion of the federal budget committed to benefit the elderly rose from 23.4 percent in 1980 to 28.2 percent ten years later (U.S. House, Committee on Ways and Means 1993, 1564). In future years, this figure was projected to increase further in response to the rapid growth of the nation's senior-citizen population and to rising health-care costs (ibid.). In addition, during the 1980s, spending on Social Security and Medicare grew as a percentage of federal spending on entitlement programs, and by 1990 it accounted for 60 percent of such expenditures (ibid., 1764–65).

Within the federal budget, Social Security's relative immunity from deficit-reduction efforts further heightened perceptions of the political power of senior citizens. Indeed, during the 1980s (with the notable exception of 1983) most in Congress were afraid to discuss even the possibility of slightly slowing the program's rapid rate of growth. (Between 1979 and 1986, spending for Old Age Survivors Insurance [OASI] virtually

6. Specific instances of elderly voters and interest groups asserting significant political influence are difficult to pinpoint. The elderly do not vote as a monolithic block; their votes are distributed in a manner similar to younger age-groups (Binstock 1987, 4–6; 1983, 138–39). Further, as Binstock (1987, 7–8) notes, senior-citizen interest groups "have had little to do with the enactment and amendment of major old age policies such as Social Security and Medicare." Instead, their influence "has been largely confined to minor policies." Nevertheless, the elderly and their political representatives have one significant form of latent political power, referred to by Binstock (1987, 10) as the "electoral bluff": politicians dare not propose or support policies inimical to the interests of senior citizens for fear of antagonizing and possibly mobilizing such a potentially potent political force.

doubled in absolute dollars, to $177 billion.) The few legislators who did attempt to address the issue found their efforts denounced by senior-citizen advocates and ignored by their colleagues.[7]

Nevertheless, during the 1980s, concerns that the elderly were consuming more than their fair share of federal resources began to be voiced increasingly by a number of journalists and academics. The phenomenon of rising economic well-being of seniors during a period when an increasing portion of federal expenditures was focused on them led such observers to question whether government resources should be diverted to more-deserving purposes and claimants. The most radical of these observers sought to discuss the issue in a framework of "intergenerational equity" (Peterson and Howe 1988; Longman 1987).[8] While the overwhelming majority of academics explicitly rejected this perspective (Marmor, Mashaw, and Harvey 1990; Kingson, Hirshorn, and Harootyan 1986), a number did criticize the relative inequity in federal resources allocated to the elderly vis-à-vis children (Hewlett 1991; Preston 1984). Cook and Barrett (1992, 230), who conducted interviews with fifty-eight members of the U.S. House of Representatives on social welfare issues, clarify this perspective:

> Representatives are not saying that federal resource distribution between the young and old is a zero-sum game such that giving to the young entails taking from the old. Rather they are simply saying that federal efforts since the 1950s have had the effect of reducing poverty among elderly Americans and the need now is to give a higher priority to children, the age group most likely to live in poor families.

By the end of the 1980s, it was the growing federal deficit, rather than any political backlash or reassessment of priorities, that limited senior-citizen political influence. With deficits running in excess of $200 billion, the power wielded by age-based interest groups appeared to be highly circumscribed, pertaining more to protecting established programs than to expanding existing ones (Binstock 1987).

7. For one example, see *Wall Street Journal*, June 17, 1987.
8. Regarding this issue, Jacobs (1990, 357) writes that "conflict or potential conflict among generations" had become "a major theme in the politics of aging" by the 1980s.

Anxiety About Rising Health-Care Costs
for Senior Citizens

Despite the gains of the preceding two decades with respect to economic well-being and political power, the affluence of senior citizens during the late 1980s was by no means universal. Significant subgroups of the elderly—particularly the so-called "oldest-old" (age 85 and over) and single persons, mainly widows—disproportionately survived on incomes below or near the poverty line. Further, while home-equity wealth was widespread among the elderly and a potential source of income for many, most seniors did not have large amounts of liquid assets (Jacobs 1986a, 34).

The chief concern of senior citizens during this period undoubtedly involved the possibility of unanticipated and substantial bills for health-care costs and other services. In 1984 the elderly paid out-of-pocket (not including Medicare Part B or private insurance premiums) more than 25 percent of their health-care bills, or $1,059 per capita.[9] In the same year, mean out-of-pocket payments (including insurance premiums) by senior citizens as a percentage of mean income stood at 15 percent, a rate identical to that of 1966, the year before Medicare was implemented. But this average was deceptive. Two-thirds of the elderly poor, and 96 percent of those with the highest incomes, spent less than 5 percent of their incomes on health care. Consequently, the lion's share of health-care costs were incurred by an unfortunate minority of seniors (Jacobs 1986a, 35).

A major reason for this phenomenon had to do with the remaining gaps in the Medicare program. Medicare protection against out-of-pocket costs varied greatly, depending on the length and degree of illness and services required (U.S. Senate, Committee on Finance 1987, pt. 1, 38–41, 43). The most comprehensive coverage was supplied by Medicare Part A, hospital insurance. In 1984 the program covered 74.8 percent of such costs, a reflection of the fact that only a very small percentage of seniors (0.7 percent in 1983) exceeded the sixty-day limit on hospital stays and became liable for co-payments. An even smaller percentage of elderly, 0.02 percent in 1985, exhausted their lifetime reserve days under Medicare, thus becom-

9. This represented significant progress relative to 1966, the year before Medicare was implemented, when seniors incurred 53.2 percent of their total health bill in out-of-pocket expenses.

ing liable for all hospital expenses beyond this period (U.S. Senate, Committee on Finance 1987, pt. 1, 38).

Medicare Part B, supplementary medical insurance, covered 57.8 percent of costs for physician services in 1984. In contrast to Medicare Part A, co-payments (equivalent to 20 percent of physician charges) in Part B occurred at the front end of the program, after the beneficiary had paid a $75 yearly deductible. As a result, a significant majority of beneficiaries—60 percent in 1986—incurred co-payment liabilities for physician services.

Although offering significant coverage for hospital stays and physician services, Medicare provided no coverage of the costs of many health-related services utilized by the elderly—such as prescription drugs, eye exams, and dental care. The major gap in Medicare, however, was its failure to cover long-term care. Medicare coverage was limited to short-term post-hospital stays in skilled nursing facilities (SNFs). As a result, in 1984, Medicare covered only 2.1 percent of elderly nursing home costs.

In an attempt to protect themselves against many out-of-pocket costs for expenses not covered by Medicare, approximately 70 percent of the senior citizens held supplemental health insurance policies, known popularly as "Medigap" plans. About half of all Medigap policies were provided on a group basis, many through retirees' former employers, while approximately half were purchased individually (U.S. House, Committee on Ways and Means, Subcommittee on Health 1987, 246). Depending on the benefit package and a policy's loss ratio (the percentage of premiums returned to policyholders as benefits), premiums ranged from $150 to $1,500 a year.

While the coverage offered by such policies varied, virtually all paid co-insurance costs associated with acute hospital stays and physician services. Further, policies generally paid 90 percent or more of the costs of acute-care hospital stays extending 365 days beyond the period covered by Medicare. Many also provided "first dollar" coverage by picking up the Medicare Part A and B deductibles. Only a small number of such policies provided any coverage for such items as prescription drugs and other services, and virtually none provided coverage for long-term care (ibid., 256–57).

In an attempt to protect the elderly from substandard and overpriced Medigap policies, Congress amended the Social Security Act in June 1980 to provide standards for policies marketed as Medigap insurance. These provisions, commonly known as the Baucus Amendments—after their principal architect, Montana Senator Max Baucus—set criminal penalties for abusive sales practices, provided requirements for minimum coverage of benefits, and, most important, established minimum standards for loss ratios (a minimum of 60 percent for individual policies, 75 percent for group policies). In 1986, a General Accounting Office study found that the Baucus Amendments were meeting their objectives (General Accounting Office 1986). A 1987 survey by Market Facts, on behalf of the Health Insurance Association of America, found generally high levels of satisfaction with the policies among elderly purchasers (ibid.).

Despite these findings, supplemental policies remained unpopular among a number of liberal members of Congress and interest groups, who denounced both the policies themselves and the concept of market-based health insurance generally as inefficient and as delivering less value for consumers' money than a federally based system of coverage would (ibid., 229–43; U.S. Senate, Committee on Finance 1987, pt. 3, 90–101). Their specific criticisms were threefold.

First, even in the presence of the Baucus Amendments, Medigap opponents continued to attack the loss ratios of such policies as too low, noting that costs of administration, marketing, and profits still consumed up to 40 percent (and sometimes more) of premiums paid by elderly policyholders. By contrast, they pointed out that Medicare's administrative costs amounted to, at most, 3 percent of revenues.

Second, Medigap opponents complained of continuing fraud and abuse in the sales and marketing of such policies. Cited were instances of salespeople inducing seniors to purchase worthless duplicative coverage, exaggerating the coverage offered by such policies, and misrepresenting themselves as being from government agencies or independent senior-citizen organizations.

From the perspective of Medigap's critics, many senior citizens continued to purchase duplicate and low-value policies because they generally failed to understand an often confusing public-private system of health care. "Medicare," charged one critic, "is an impossible maze, defeating even the most educated consumers. . . . Adding to this confusion, consumers must comprehend a variety of private policies marketed to the elderly (often through deceptive marketing techniques)" (U.S. Senate, Committee on Finance 1987, pt. 3, 95–96). As evidence, they cited research (McCall, Rice, and Sangl 1986) indicating that senior citizens had a relatively low level of knowledge with respect to Medicare and private insurance.

Third, and perhaps most important, is that even though 70 percent of senior citizens possessed supplementary policies (an unspecified number receiving such coverage free or partially subsidized as part of retirement benefits), a modest but significant proportion, many of whom had low incomes, held no such coverage. Among the elderly not covered by such policies, between one-third and one-half (approximately 10 to 15 percent of the total elderly population) received comparable protection through Medicaid, the federal health-care program serving the poor. The remaining group, 15 to 20 percent of all elderly, had neither public nor private supplementary insurance coverage. According to a study financed by the Health Care Financing Administration, about half of beneficiaries who had no supplemental protection said they simply could not afford it (U.S. House, Committee on Ways and Means, Subcommittee on Health 1987, 247,257).

A study by the Congressional Budget Office (CBO) confirmed that low-income beneficiaries were the most likely to lack supplemental coverage (Medigap insurance or Medicaid), noting that only 44 percent of the elderly with incomes below $5,000 had supplemental coverage, versus 87 percent of those with incomes above $25,000. At the same time, the study reported that Medicaid covered only 28 percent of the low-income group, leaving 29 percent with no coverage at all. By comparison, only 10 percent of the $25,000+ group lacked any coverage (ibid., 157). Proponents of supplemental insurance agreed with critics that the existence of this uncovered population was problematic, but they believed that solutions should rely on efforts to expand supplemental private insurance to those lacking it, rather than on attempts to supplant the marketplace with a government-administered system (ibid., 255–59, 282–85).

While out-of-pocket costs resulting from acute-care hospitalizations, physician services, and other items, such as prescription drugs, constituted areas of continuing concern for the elderly and policy-makers alike, the most daunting catastrophic health expenses facing senior citizens were those arising from a long-term chronic illness. Indeed, among the elderly who incurred out-of-pocket health-care expenses in excess of $2,000 yearly, long-term care accounted for more than 80 percent of such costs (ibid., 141).

In 1985, some 5 percent of senior citizens—1.4 million persons—resided in nursing homes. Although half of nursing-home admissions were for less than 90 days, the average length of stay for all nursing-home stays was 456 days. Indeed, for residents staying at least 90 days, the average length of stay was 830 days (U.S. Senate, Committee on Finance, Subcommittee on Health 1987, 191). As a result, one study (Cohen et al. 1986) found that "only a very small percentage of entrants [to nursing homes], 14–17 percent, account for about two-thirds of all nursing home expenditures."

With Medicare and the Medigap policies purchased by most elderly providing virtually no coverage for long-term care, those requiring such services paid more than 40 percent of total costs out-of-pocket. Because a twelve-month stay in a nursing home cost in excess of $20,000, even a brief stay could mean significant financial hardship, and a longer stay could lead to impoverishment. For example, a 1985 study by the House Aging Committee found that approximately two-thirds of single older persons and one-third of older couples in Massachusetts were impoverished after only thirteen weeks in a nursing home (U.S. House, Committee on Ways and Means, Subcommittee on Health 1987, 147). In fact, the federal government paid a significant share of long-term care costs—42 percent— through Medicaid, the health-care program for the poor. However, to be eligible for such coverage, individuals were first compelled to "spend down" income and assets to state-established eligibility levels.

While many elderly incorrectly believed that Medicare or Medigap insurance covered long-term care (McCall, Rice, and Sangl 1986), those who knew better were terrified by the prospect of losing everything they had earned during their lifetimes in order to qualify for Medicaid coverage. Despite these fears, virtually none of the elderly held private insurance for long-term care, and few such policies existed. The main obstacle to large-scale purchase of long-term-care insurance concerned cost. Because people age 65 and over constituted a high-risk population (considerably more likely to require long-term care than younger age-groups), premiums were set beyond affordability for all but the wealthiest elderly (Pepper Commission 1990, 104–10).

By the late 1980s, then, the vast majority of seniors had significant coverage for many of the costs associated with health-care expenses through Medicare and supplemental Medigap insurance. Nevertheless, rapidly rising medical costs, as well as the continuing absence of protection in numerous areas (from acute hospital stays to long-term nursing-home care), came to be a cause for increased anxiety among senior citizens. How policy-makers sought to respond to such concerns in an era of budgetary limits is the subject of the next two chapters.

2

EVOLUTION OF THE MCCA

In February 1983 President Reagan proposed a restructuring of Medicare's Hospital Insurance program to pay for unlimited costs associated with acute-care hospital stays. The proposal was criticized and rejected by congressional Democrats. Because the plan's added co-insurance far exceeded those necessary to pay for long-term acute hospital stays, opponents charged that the proposal was little more than a thinly veiled effort to reduce Medicare costs. There was a degree of truth to this. Under the plan, beneficiaries using hospital services would pay an extra $250 in 1984. The administration estimated that this would save an estimated $4.1 billion in Medicare spending over three years (U.S. Senate, Committee on Finance 1987, pt. 1, 61).

Perhaps more important, however, was the criticism that the restructuring would benefit only a handful of Medicare beneficiaries (0.7 percent in 1983), at the expense of increased co-payments for millions who had relatively brief hospital stays (Thompson 1990, 67–68). Of course, this criticism was ironic given that insurance typically functions to accomplish precisely this end.

The issue of Medicare coverage for catastrophic health expenses would have remained dormant without the efforts of Otis Bowen, who was nominated to become Secretary of the Department of Health and Human Services in November 1985. A former family physician and Republican governor from Indiana, Bowen took the post with the issue and a proposed solution at the top of his agenda. According to popular accounts, Bowen's interest in catastrophic coverage originated during a three-month hospitalization of his first wife for bone cancer (from which she later died). Bowen was said to have been dismayed by the increasing co-payments Medicare required of people who had lengthy acute hospital stays (Longman 1989, 16).

Bowen's involvement with the issue increased when, in 1982, he was selected by President Reagan to head the Advisory Council on Social Security. Although the council's main task was "to examine the fiscal integrity" of Medicare's trust fund and come up with alternatives for improving it, "Bowen devoted considerable time to a proposal that would expand Medicare coverage for acute hospital care" (Englund 1988, 27; see also Thompson 1990, chap. 3). Even though about seven of ten Medicare beneficiaries held Medigap coverage covering many of the costs associated with acute hospital stays, Bowen was said to be disenchanted with the low loss ratios of these policies (the percentage of premiums returned to policyholders as benefits), which often failed to exceed the 60 to 70 percent range (Englund 1988, 27).

Following Bowen's lead, the council eventually approved a proposal restructuring and expanding Medicare Part A to cover all costs for unlimited acute hospital stays. Similar to Reagan's 1983 proposal, the plan would pay for these benefits by instituting daily co-insurance equal to 3 percent of the inpatient deductible for all inpatient days (except those subject to the deductible). It is important to note, however, that Medicare beneficiaries would be permitted to purchase coverage for hospital co-insurance costs through Part B of the Medicare program. The additional benefits were to be financed through premiums estimated to cost each beneficiary approximately $42 yearly.

In 1985 Bowen built on the council's proposal by adding an out-of-pocket limit on costs for physician services. Like the earlier plan, costs would also be paid by flat premiums levied on beneficiaries. Bowen set forth this proposal in the November–December 1985 issue of the *Federation of American Hospitals Review* with Thomas Burke, who had served as the council's executive director and eventually became his chief-of-staff at the Department of Health and Human Services. It would ultimately serve as the prototype for the Reagan administration's proposal on catastrophic care.

Because Bowen's plan to expand Medicare essentially usurped an area covered by most Medigap policies, his ideas on this issue were probably anathema to political conservatives wielding influence with the Reagan administration. Nevertheless, Bowen's views on this matter were apparently disregarded in the decision to nominate him for the Health and Human

Services post. Instead, he seems to have been selected for reasons having little to do with ideology (Thompson 1990, 106, 119). Bowen was said to fulfill White House Chief-of-Staff Donald Regan's desire for a quiet, competent administrator who would be loyal to administration policies. Indeed, from all appearances, Bowen was a nonideological politician who eschewed controversy and could be easily handled by senior administration officials. He was also popular with Democrats and Republicans in Congress, so his cabinet-post nomination would be confirmed easily.

According to Kingdon (1984), the defining characteristic of policy entrepreneurs is the "willingness to invest their resources—time, energy, reputation, and sometimes money—in the hope of future return." With his confirmation as Secretary of Health and Human Services, Bowen, possessing all but the last of these resources and occupying a position of influence, assumed this role completely. Almost immediately he began lobbying hard to include a catastrophic-care initiative in President Reagan's 1986 State of the Union Address.

Early in Bowen's tenure, a number of influential White House aides became convinced that the issue had political appeal. With mid-term elections less than a year away, surveys conducted by pollster Richard Wirthlin had found Reagan to be particularly unpopular with the elderly. Adoption of catastrophic health-care coverage as an issue, he believed, would "soften" the President's image among this group of crucial voters (Englund 1988, 28). In addition, an administration initiative was believed likely to preempt congressional action on the issue. White House Political Adviser Mitch Daniels was aware that a number of lawmakers were planning to introduce catastrophic-care legislation. By initiating a proposal first, he believed, the administration would be able to minimize the scope of such legislation (Thompson 1990, 127; Englund 1988, 27–28).

These arguments, in combination with Bowen's personal lobbying of Reagan and other administration officials, were initially persuasive. At first the President agreed not only to announce his support for the broad concept of catastrophic legislation in his 1986 State of the Union Address, but also to include a promise to introduce legislation that same year (Thompson 1990, 123–24). When administration conservatives and representatives of the insurance industry learned of these plans, however, they immediately attacked them as a thinly veiled effort by Bowen to expand Medicare at the expense of a competently functioning Medigap industry. The protests caused Reagan to back away from his intention to introduce catastrophic-care legislation in 1986. Instead, in his State of the Union Address, Reagan ordered Bowen to conduct a study of the issue and develop a proposal based on its findings (Thompson 1990, 124–27).

Although suspicious of Bowen, administration conservatives were initially relieved at this outcome. They believed that Bowen's study of the issue would produce a variety of options for catastrophic care, which would include his own as well as a number of market-oriented proposals to expand Medigap coverage. The report would offer the White House an opportunity to choose a proposal that was in accord with Reagan's true preferences on the issue (Thompson 1990, 160–61). Since Reagan was believed to favor a private-sector initiative (Englund 1988, 28), administration conservatives foresaw that the study process would lead to adoption of an alternative favorable to them. Only later did they see that they had miscalculated, for events soon showed that Bowen had little intention of conducting a study endorsing any plan but his own.[1]

By outward appearances, Bowen proceeded to conduct the Reagan-ordered study in an impartial manner. At the first meeting of an advisory council of sub-cabinet-level appointees charged with studying the issue, he announced that the final report would not be simply a rubber stamp of his previous catastrophic-care proposal (Thompson 1990, 140). Bowen declined to attend other meetings of the advisory council, ostensibly to allow the committee to work its will uninfluenced by his presence. During 1986, well-publicized hearings were held throughout the nation to allow representatives of business, consumer groups, state agencies, providers, policy researchers, and labor unions to state their views on catastrophic care as well as on other health-care-related issues (Thompson 1990, 153; Englund 1988, 28).

Behind this veneer of fact-finding, however, Bowen engaged in political hardball. Working through his chief-of-staff, Thomas Burke, Bowen sought to exclude anyone who was likely to oppose his plan. During the spring and summer of 1986, the views of those urging private-sector alternatives to the Bowen plan (such as vouchers for those lacking such insurance) were systematically dismissed, ignored, or overruled (Thompson 1990, 170–72). At the same time, Bowen also refused to endorse any proposal, particularly

1. Thompson (1990, 137) writes that those who knew of Bowen's work on the 1982 Social Security Advisory Council, and his *FAH Review* article, understood that the Reagan-ordered study was "an exercise designed to endorse the catastrophic care recommendations of the Commission." Apparently, many in the administration were unfamiliar with Bowen's record on the issue, or disregarded the significance of such information.

his own, probably fearing that doing so would mobilize White House conservatives to undermine the study. Finally, in late October 1986, three weeks before the study deadline, Bowen ordered advisers to include his catastrophic-care plan. Developed from the proposal set forth in his *FAH Review* article with Burke, Bowen's proposal sought to extend Medicare protection to acute hospital and physician costs in excess of $2,000 yearly. The expansion was to be financed by a flat $4.92 monthly premium levied on all Medicare recipients.

On November 19 Bowen revealed his proposal to the White House Domestic Policy Council. His presentation was met with heavy opposition by Attorney General Ed Meese, Council of Economic Advisers Chair Beryl Sprinkel, and Office of Management and Budget Director James Miller (Englund 1990, 28; Thompson 1990, 189). The criticisms of these and other conservatives were essentially threefold. First, in their view, the Bowen plan sought to replace a competently functioning private market with a government monopoly. If a modest proportion of the elderly held no supplemental coverage, they believed that the government should provide vouchers for the purchase of such coverage, not dismantle the Medigap industry. The second criticism concerned the Bowen plan's costs. Conservatives argued that since Medicare's creation program costs had consistently exceeded even the most generous projections. Although the Bowen plan was to be financed completely by monthly premiums paid by beneficiaries, conservatives predicted that costs were likely to escalate more rapidly than the willingness of senior citizens to pay increased premiums. When this occurred, interest groups representing seniors would exert political pressure to fund the program through general revenues. Third, conservatives feared that the Democratic Congress and lobbies for the elderly would exploit the Bowen plan by using it as a vehicle for expanding Medicare coverage for other items, such as prescription drugs and certain types of nursing-home care. The result would be a legislative "Christmas tree" that would probably dwarf the cost of the Bowen plan.

In the belief that opponents planned to squelch or undermine his report, Bowen decided to release it as soon as possible. Consequently, even as the White House Office of Legislative Affairs was telling Department of Health and Human Services officials not to discuss the plan with anyone until Reagan had decided whether to endorse it, Bowen scheduled a news conference for November 20. The maneuver was a clever one—because canceling the press conference would create an uproar, the White House had no choice but to allow it to proceed (Englund 1988, 28; Lambro 1987).

Bowen unveiled his proposal to a chorus of praise from Democrats in Congress as well as senior-citizen interest groups, such as AARP. Indeed, Reagan's political opponents appeared to relish the idea of an administration appointee urging an expansion of federal health insurance. Senator Edward Kennedy, long an advocate of national health insurance, chided Republican leaders in Congress "to listen a little more" to Bowen and "a little less to the insurance lobby" (Lambro 1987). Bowen's press conference precipitated a spate of activity on Capitol Hill as legislators set off to write their own versions of catastrophic-care legislation. By January 1987 eight proposals had been introduced in the House, while six members of the Senate Finance Committee were said to be at work on similar legislation. As this occurred, members of Congress announced their intention to pass legislation even in the absence of a Reagan endorsement of the Bowen plan (Thompson 1990, 217).

By raising expectations in Congress and the media, the release of the Bowen plan increased pressure on the President to endorse it. If Reagan were to reject the proposal, he would be forced to justify disagreement with a study he had ordered. The ensuing media coverage and reaction would probably prove embarrassing.

Still, for all of Bowen's efforts, a presidential endorsement of his proposal was far from certain. Indeed, by January 1987 the conventional wisdom in Washington held that the Bowen plan had little chance of winning Reagan's approval (Thompson 1990, 204). Of course, such views amounted to little more than conjecture. No one really knew what Ronald Reagan believed about the issue. At the same time, those familiar with the political proclivities of Reagan and his administration were correctly skeptical about the prospects of the Bowen plan. After all, the President was the head of an administration that was ideologically committed to free enterprise and to reducing, not expanding, the size of government.

Moreover, following the release of the Bowen report, administration conservatives at last began to assert themselves on the issue. Led by Ed Meese, they organized to attack the Bowen proposal and replace it with a market-based alternative of their own. In their view, Reagan could not be permitted to endorse the Bowen plan without a fight, which in fact is what ensued between December 1986 and February 1987. During this period, a series of increasingly acrimonious White House meetings were held to debate the issue of health-care coverage for acute catastrophic illness (Thompson 1990, chaps. 6–7).

Although promising in the abstract, conservative efforts to develop an alternative to the Bowen plan quickly stumbled. The Medigap industry was prohibited by law from covering hospital expenses beyond a 365-day period after the insured person exhausted Medicare benefits. In an attempt to make Medigap policies competitive with the Bowen plan, conservatives proposed that the regulation be changed in order to make them truly acute-care catastrophic (that is, permitting them to cover expenses beyond the 365-day period).

To their surprise, however, representatives of the insurance industry balked at providing this coverage, arguing that doing so would render Medigap policies unprofitable in the absence of significant premium increases (Englund 1988, 28–30; Thompson 1990, 198–99; see also Prokesch 1987). As a result, insurers were willing to cede this function to the federal government rather than include it as part of standard policies.

The disinclination or inability of insurers to match the Bowen plan in terms of costs and benefits essentially doomed the efforts of conservatives to develop a market-based alternative. Although they continued to argue on behalf of such an approach throughout January and February 1987, their efforts to counter the Bowen plan came to be largely confined to criticisms of its costs and potential for evolving into "Christmas tree" legislation. Despite the absence of a credible alternative, many conservatives continued to believe that Reagan could be ultimately persuaded to reject the Bowen plan. According to Englund (1988, 30), "They were convinced that at the last minute, Ed Meese could look the President in the eye and say 'Don't do it.' "

However, although this scenario could have transpired at another time, events of the period intervened to benefit the Bowen plan (Thompson 1990, 184–88, 204–12). First, in mid-term elections of November 1986, Democrats regained control of the Senate for the first time since 1980. Emboldened by the victory, Democrats vowed to utilize their legislative majorities in Congress to participate in policy-making as an equal partner with the President. Second, following the elections the Reagan administration was further weakened by the unfolding Iran-Contra scandal. Involving an administration-sponsored attempt to trade arms to Iran for the release of hostages held in Lebanon, and the diversion of profits to aid the Nicaraguan rebels, the affair resulted in a torrent of news coverage that was critical of the Reagan White House. Questions concerning Reagan's ability to govern increased further in January 1987, when he appeared to recover slowly from prostate surgery.

As these events caused Reagan's popularity to plummet, the White House struggled to find an issue that would steer the political focus away from the administration's problems. The Bowen plan, a limited but significant reform likely to meet with approval by the Democratic Congress, provided such a vehicle. On January 28, 1987, Bowen made a series of appearances before congressional committees to tout his proposal. He was treated as a visionary and a hero (Thompson 1990, 214–15), and congressmen also used the occasion to scold Reagan for his indecision and to threaten to enact legislation without White House input if an initiative did not arrive soon.

With Congress clamoring for action by the administration, with conservatives unable to produce a credible alternative, and with the White House eager to demonstrate that it was not paralyzed by recent events, Reagan finally endorsed the Bowen plan on February 12, 1987. In announcing his support, the President said he was "asking Congress to help give Americans that last full measure of security, to provide a health insurance plan that fights the fear of catastrophic illness" (*New York Times* 1987a). He further described the plan as "a giant step forward" in helping people who must now "make a choice between financial ruin and death."

In contrast to this rhetoric, the plan Reagan had adopted as his own was in actuality what it had always been—a simple, budget-neutral, limited expansion of Medicare. Indeed, Reagan's reference to the plan as protection against the costs of "catastrophic care" was a misnomer, for it provided no coverage for a number of significant medical expenses, including prescription drugs and, most significant, long-term care.

Nevertheless, Reagan's endorsement of the Bowen plan was significant because it marked the culmination of the Health and Human Services secretary's efforts to put the issue on the political agenda. The Bowen proposal was received by a Democratic Congress that was eager to enact proactive legislation affecting Medicare after years of retrenchment. "This was the first time in seven years such an opportunity presented itself," commented one congressional staffer interviewed, which explains the enthusiasm among officials of senior-citizen interest groups and supporters in Congress for the chance to increase Medicare's scope. Over the next several months, Congress would labor hard to exploit the opening presented by the Reagan proposal.

Before Reagan endorsed the Bowen plan, it received virtually universal praise from congressional Democrats and representatives of senior-citizen interest groups. Once Reagan adopted it, however, the proposal was harshly criticized by many of the same people as constituting a largely superficial and cosmetic effort to improve Medicare. "The President calls this a giant step forward," said Representative Claude Pepper, chairman of the House Rules Committee and the leading advocate for seniors in Congress. "This isn't a step taken by a giant. It's one taken by a pygmy" (Rovner 1987a, 297). Representative Henry Waxman, chairman of the House Energy and Commerce Committee's Subcommittee on Health and the Environment, concurred, calling the plan "a hoax." He added, "With its limited gesture of assistance, the administration has come upon a car wreck and changed only a tire" (Rovner 1987a, 434). Ronald Pollack, executive director of Villers Advocacy Associates (later called Families U.S.A.), a group promoting the interests of low-income seniors, was equally harsh in his assessment terming the proposal "hype" and "much ado about very little" (Pollack 1987).

The underlying cause of these criticisms concerned the Reagan plan's failure to include Medicare coverage for long-term care. By 1987 this issue was preeminent in the agendas of senior-citizen interest groups and their supporters in Congress. In fact, as the President's plan was introduced, officials of the AARP and Villers were laying the groundwork for "Long-Term Care '88," a campaign aimed at educating the public and political candidates on the issue. While the effort was ostensibly limited to consciousness-raising activities about long-term care generally, organizers undoubtedly hoped that its major by-product would be increased public support for a federally funded long-term-care program. Eventually supported by more than one hundred national organizations, "Long-Term Care '88" was to provide the focus for political activities of advocates for the aging through that year's elections and beyond (Davidson 1988; Rovner 1988c, 939).

During the 100th Congress, this campaign was complemented by Claude Pepper's attempt to win passage of major long-term-care legislation, or at least make government inaction an election issue. The most significant of his efforts, H.R. 3436 (sponsored with House Select Aging Committee Chairman Ed Roybal), sought to establish a long-term home-care benefit for anyone whom a physician certified as needing assistance with two or more of the recognized activities of daily living (bathing, eating, dressing, etc.).[2] The program was to be financed by lifting the $43,800 income payroll cap on the 1.45 percent Medicare payroll tax.

2. Pepper's legislation was originally introduced as H.R. 2762. In November 1987 Pepper used his power as chairman of the House Rules Committee to insert the text of this first bill into a minor measure, H.R. 3436, as a means of expediting floor action on the legislation (Rovner 1987j, 2874).

A number of factors combined to make the Pepper bill highly controversial. First, many legislators believed that its imposition of costs almost solely on younger generations was inequitable and constituted a significant tax increase on such persons. A significant number of legislators also worried that the costs of the benefits included in the legislation would quickly outstrip revenues. Finally, Representatives Dan Rostenkowski and John Dingell, respectively chairmen of the House Committee on Ways and Means and the House Committee on Energy and Commerce, complained that Pepper was overstepping his authority by seeking to bring the bill directly to the House floor without input from their committees (Rovner 1988f, 1491–93).

Had it been introduced by any other member of Congress, the "Pepper bill" would have stood no chance of passage, but Pepper was no ordinary congressman. By 1987, the eighty-six-year-old representative wielded considerable power as chairman of the Committee on Rules and by virtue of his legendary reputation as the nation's most visible champion of senior-citizen interests. During the 100th Congress, Pepper and his supporters mounted a substantial effort to win passage of his long-term home-care proposal. By the time the Pepper bill was debated in June 1988, it was co-sponsored by more than 150 House members and supported by more than ninety health, children's, senior citizens', and social service organizations.

Although the above-mentioned concerns would lead the House in June 1988 to reject H.R. 3436 by a vote of 243 to 169, Pepper's efforts on the bill's behalf would influence significantly the content of the catastrophic-care legislation that emerged from Congress (Rovner 1987g, 1591). (Ultimately, his actions would also influence the decisions of many rank-and-file members to support the measure; see Chapter 4.) Throughout 1987 and the first six months of 1988, Pepper continually threatened to offer his long-term home-care proposal as an amendment to the catastrophic-care bill, as a means of prodding those developing the legislation to expand its scope.[3] Because the addition of such an amendment would almost certainly

3. On July 9, 1987, shortly before the House vote on the catastrophic-care legislation, Pepper reluctantly backed away from this idea under pressure from House Speaker Jim Wright. In exchange, Wright promised Pepper a floor vote on his bill following the final House vote on catastrophic care. When conference committee negotiations on the catastrophic-care legislation proceeded slowly in the early months of 1988, Pepper threatened to renege on this agreement, warning that he and his supporters were "getting to the edge of our indulgence" waiting to bring his legislation to the floor. With Pepper "breathing down their necks," conferees raced to finish work on the legislation, resolving their differences late in May 1988 (Rovner 1988e, 1402).

bring a Reagan veto and probably death for the legislation as a whole, those in Congress with jurisdiction over catastrophic care had little choice but to expand the benefits their bill offered in order to placate Pepper and his supporters. Thus, even if passage of his long-term-care legislation was not to occur in the 100th Congress, Pepper would use his bill as a tool to pressure Congress to close as many of the gaps in Medicare as possible.

Although eager to accommodate many of the demands for expanded benefits, legislators with jurisdiction over Medicare initially proceeded cautiously in their efforts to build on the Reagan plan. This was mainly the result of one powerful fiscal constraint: the political necessity of financing such legislation solely through payments of beneficiaries themselves (see Chapter 3). In the words of one congressman, this requirement was to impose "a powerful discipline" on lawmakers who were developing catastrophic-care proposals (Pear 1987b).

On February 27 the first of these efforts emerged in a proposal co-authored by Representatives Fortney H. "Pete" Stark and Bill Gradison, respectively chairman and ranking member of the House Ways and Means Health Subcommittee. The plan capped the amount beneficiaries would pay for hospital and physician costs at roughly $1,700 yearly, $300 less than the Reagan plan. It is significant that the plan also included a one-deductible maximum for beneficiaries who had multiple hospital stays during a particular year. (Under the Reagan plan, beneficiaries were liable for costs of the first-day deductible for up to three separate stays.) In addition, Stark-Gradison extended coverage for care in skilled nursing facilities (SNFs) from 100 to 150 days, reduced co-insurance costs, and transferred them to the first seven days of care. The plan's benefits were to be financed through taxation of the subsidized portion of Medicare benefits.

While commending Stark-Gradison as an improvement on the Reagan plan, advocates for the elderly viewed the proposal as merely "a useful foundation upon which to build." Elaborating in March 4 testimony before the Ways and Means Health Subcommittee, AARP President John Denning testified that, despite advancing "the evolutionary movement towards a more comprehensive catastrophic protection package," the "modest benefit improvements" contained in Stark-Gradison failed to justify the plan's radically changed financing mechanism (U.S. House, Committee on Ways and Means, Subcommittee on Health 1987, 151–52). Pepper also appeared before the committee to appeal for more comprehensive legislation. "If we pass up this opportunity," he said, "we may not come around to this again for another 20 years" (Rovner 1987b, 434).

While sympathetic to such appeals, Stark and Gradison warned that those seeking to expand their plan risked undermining it by making it prone to a Reagan veto. "It's important as we work on this issue that we don't blow it by trying to do too much," said Gradison. Stark concurred, saying, "When you get Gradison and me and Bowen and the President together, you better reserve one of those puppies, because you're not likely to get a breeding like that again soon" (Rovner 1987b, 434).

However, during March and April 1987, Stark and Gradison disregarded their own admonitions and further expanded their proposal. "Responding to intense lobbying from the AARP and other organizations" (AARP Vote 1987), the Ways and Means Health Subcommittee doubled the Medicare home health-care benefit, eliminated the requirement limiting coverage of SNF stays to those hospitalized at least three days prior to SNF admission, and required states, through Medicaid, to pay Medicare deductibles and co-insurance for people with incomes below the poverty line. This augmented Stark-Gradison proposal was approved by the subcommittee on April 9. A little more than a month later, on May 19, the bill, including a new financing mechanism relying on a combination of flat and progressive premiums, passed the full Ways and Means Committee.

As this occurred, Lloyd Bentsen, chairman of the Senate Finance Committee, introduced similar legislation. Broadly supported by the committee's Democrats and Republicans, the measure (S.1127) won quick and unanimous approval on May 9. Commenting on the close resemblance between the Bentsen and Stark-Gradison bills, the *Congressional Quarterly* reported that this was "due in large part to what both House and Senate staffers describe as 'unprecedented' bipartisan and bicameral cooperation" (Rovner 1987e, 1136).

Despite the expanded benefits contained in the Stark-Gradison and Bentsen proposals and the apparent consensus in support of them, political pressure from advocates for the elderly and from supporters in Congress resulted in the addition of more benefits to what was to become a textbook example of "Christmas tree" legislation. In May–June 1987 the impetus for new benefits materialized in the House Energy and Commerce Committee's Subcommittee on Health and the Environment, which shared jurisdiction over Medicare with Ways and Means. At the urging of its chairman, Henry Waxman, the subcommittee's version of catastrophic-care legislation included new or expanded coverage for respite care, mammograms, and protection against spousal impoverishment caused by the illness of one partner. The latter two items would later be added to the Bentsen bill, while the respite-care benefit would be accepted by the Senate in conference.

Congress added a plethora of new and expanded benefits to the Reagan plan, but none of these exemplified the growth of the legislation better than the issue of prescription-drug coverage. Initially, Bentsen, Gradison, House Ways and Means Chairman Dan Rostenkowski, and many in the administration opposed the inclusion of a drug benefit citing uncertainty over costs. In fact, such concerns were well founded. The government agencies charged with estimating the price of such a benefit possessed little reliable data concerning how much the elderly spent each year on prescription drugs, and as a result their cost estimates varied widely. For example, the 1989 cost of a House Ways and Means proposal covering 80 percent of prescription-drug expenses after an $800 deductible was pegged at $6.4 billion by the Department of Health and Human Services, but at only $750 million by Congressional Budget Office estimates (Rovner 1987f, 1328). From Gradison's perspective, this discrepancy was a sign that Congress did not have "enough facts to make an intelligent decision" on prescription drugs. When estimates are this far apart, he continued, "a lot of warning lights go off" (Rovner 1987f, 1328). "It's a pig in a poke—you don't know what you have," concurred Representative Edward Madigan, the ranking Republican on Energy and Commerce's Subcommittee on Health and the Environment (Rich 1987a).[4]

Between May and September 1987, however, those who had such concerns were overwhelmed by political pressure from the AARP and from a number of influential members of Congress on behalf of a prescription-drug benefit. From the beginning of the legislative process, the AARP had refused to endorse the principle of elderly-only financing for catastrophic care in the absence of a prescription-drug benefit. Following the failure of Stark and Gradison to include the item in their bill (Stark believed that Congress and the elderly were not willing to pay the costs of this benefit), dissatisfied representatives of the organization took their case to House Speaker Jim Wright and found a sympathetic audience (Iglehart 1989, 335). At a May 4 meeting of leading members of the Ways and Means, Energy and Commerce, and Aging committees, Wright embraced the prescription-drug benefit as a way to put a Democratic stamp on what had been a

---

4. While Bentsen was concerned about the cost of the prescription-drug benefit, he dismissed HHS's figures as "grossly exaggerated" (Rich 1987c).

Reagan initiative (Rovner 1987d, 1082). Waxman, who had already begun drafting prescription-drug legislation, inserted it in the Energy and Commerce Department's bill on May 20. With Wright's backing, Waxman's measure won rapid approval from both Energy and Commerce, and Ways and Means.

In the Senate, a bipartisan group of senators led by John Heinz and George Mitchell worked on a similar benefit to be offered as an amendment to the Bentsen bill. With Bentsen the main obstacle to Senate approval of the amendment, the AARP approached him and quickly managed to change his mind (Englund 1988, 30). Aware of the increasing momentum on behalf of a prescription-drug benefit, Bentsen offered the AARP a deal: he would support a drug amendment if it was phased in deficit-neutral with revenues more than sufficient to cover costs. Bentsen also insisted that the benefit be scaled back to constitute "truly catastrophic coverage not just a routine benefit" (Englund 1988, 30). AARP agreed, and Bentsen's endorsement in September 1987 effectively guaranteed that a prescription-drug benefit would be included in the Senate bill.

At first appearance, these developments appeared to make the legislation vulnerable to a veto; between February and July 1987 the Reagan administration was on record as opposing a drug benefit, because of reservations about the cost. Shortly after Reagan's endorsement of his catastrophic-care proposal, Secretary Bowen had declared that he would recommend a veto of any legislation containing such a provision (*New York Times* 1987b). On June 15, shortly after a drug benefit was inserted in the House bill, Bowen reiterated this threat (Englund 1988, 30). Just over a month later, on July 21, four senior administration officials, including Bowen, sent a letter to House Speaker Wright opposing the drug benefit and warning of a presidential veto if the House included it in the final legislation (Englund 1988, 30).

The following day, Reagan himself had endorsed this position, vowing to veto the legislation in a closed meeting with Republican congressional leaders. Following House passage of its bill including a prescription-drug benefit on July 22, Reagan escalated his attack on the legislation. In his July 26 radio address he accused House Democrats of more than tripling the costs of the Bowen plan and warned that "in about fifteen years" the program would "run a $20 billion dollar deficit and threaten the solvency of the entire Medicare trust fund" (Pear 1987c).

Despite the repeated warnings and rhetoric of Reagan and other administration officials, the White House actually had little resolve to oppose any of the legislation's new benefits, including prescription drugs. Throughout the summer of 1987, the administration remained weakened by and preoccupied with the continuing Iran-Contra scandal as Congress held nationally televised hearings investigating its role. In such an environment, the White House did not have the energy or will to pick a fight with Congress over issues as mundane as prescription drugs. In addition, Bowen, while concerned about the costs of this benefit, was likely eager to avert a veto of legislation he had fathered.

As a consequence, in August and September 1987 the White House entered into negotiations with Bentsen, aiming to win stricter cost constraints on the legislation in exchange for its acceptance of the prescription-drug benefit (Englund 1988, 30). Late in September, after marathon negotiations, a deal was struck. Bentsen's concessions were substantial: the out-of-pocket threshold on hospital and physician expenses was increased from $1,700 to $1,850 yearly and, more significant, was to be increased each year so that no more than 7 percent of beneficiaries exceeded the cap. The presence of these controls, which were ultimately included in the final legislation, increased the likelihood that its benefits would remain truly catastrophic, limited to those with the highest out-of-pocket medical expenses each year. Nevertheless, AARP and the advocates of the elderly in Congress considered this a fair price to pay for the long-desired prescription-drug benefit. In October 1987 the provision would be offered as an amendment to the Bentsen bill during the Senate floor debate.

The inclusion of prescription drugs with the other new benefits increased the legislation's costs precipitously. Indeed, the five-year cost of the catastrophic-care law was estimated at just below $30 billion (Congressional Budget Office 1988b), more than twice the $13 billion price tag of the Bowen plan. For Congress, paying the costs of the "Christmas tree" legislation in an era of budgetary austerity would be a major challenge.

3

FINANCING
THE MCCA PROGRAM

The Bowen plan set the parameters for financing catastrophic care. Acceptable proposals would be deficit-neutral and, more significant, paid for solely by beneficiaries themselves. Congress quickly embraced these principles in developing its own alternatives.

The consensus in Congress that new programs not be financed through deficit spending was a direct consequence of federal budget politics during this period. With yearly deficits rising into the $200 billion range by the late 1980s, even the most justifiable causes were unlikely to be championed in the absence of accompanying revenues. This sentiment was particularly strong within the two committees that had jurisdiction over catastrophic-care legislation—the House Ways and Means and Senate Finance committees.

Agreement that beneficiaries, in this case the elderly, should bear all of the legislation's costs may be explained by two factors. The first concerned Ronald Reagan himself. The President's February 1987 endorsement of the Bowen plan signaled Reagan's intention to support a politically popular benefit expansion in an election year. However, the prospect of paying for such a program even partially through new or higher taxes on nonelderly workers remained anathema to him, both ideologically and politically, and would almost certainly receive his veto. By contrast, premiums imposed on the elderly could be justified as "user fees," because all revenues collected would be used solely to finance the program's benefits (Kosterlitz 1989c, 2454). Laying aside the fact that a veto override was unlikely, congressional Democrats, eager to shake their reputation as supporters of high taxes, believed that confronting Reagan on the issue would effectively cede his party the high ground on what was likely to become a key issue in the 1988 campaign. Moreover, many in Congress viewed Reagan's endorsement of the Bowen plan as an unprecedented opportunity to pass proactive Medicare legislation, rather than an occasion to be exploited for political purposes (see Chapter 2). Consequently, Congress's acceptance of elderly-only financing represented a quid pro quo for administration support of catastrophic-care legislation.

Second, elderly-only financing was motivated by the growing realization among policy-makers that the elderly constituted an increasingly affluent segment of the population who were consuming a significant if not disproportionate share of government resources (see Chapter 1). In the words of one congressman interviewed for this study: "Demographic data show that the elderly are in better shape than the nonelderly. This is particularly true with respect to the affluent elderly. In light of this, it wasn't right to ask the nonelderly to finance their [the elderly's] benefits in the case of catastrophic care." As a result, lawmakers confronted with financing catastrophic care expressed little willingness to impose its costs on younger generations. If such a program was to be implemented, the new conventional wisdom dictated that the elderly themselves should bear the costs.

This consensus raised a second and even more delicate dilemma for Congress—how to distribute such costs among the elderly. Early on, the legislation's architects decided that the benefits should be financed in a progressive manner according to "ability-to-pay" principles. In making this choice, policy-makers were guided by two closely related impulses—one pragmatic, the other philosophical.

First, progressive financing provided the additional revenues necessary to finance the legislation's expanded benefits without unduly burdening low-income senior citizens. A chief complaint about the Bowen plan had concerned its flat-premium method of financing, under which all seniors—rich and poor—would pay an identical $4.92 premium each month. Because such premiums would represent a greater burden to those with low incomes, critics decried the mechanism as inequitable. "It is as if the owners of a $20,000 rundown hovel were to be charged the same fire insurance premium to protect their home as were the owners of a $2 million mansion," said Ronald Pollack of Villers Advocacy Associates in reference to the Bowen plan's method of financing (U.S. House, Committee on Ways and Means, Subcommittee on Health 1987, 176).

The unacceptability of flat-premium financing only increased further as expansion of catastrophic-care benefits by Congress more than doubled the cost of its legislation relative to the Bowen plan. If $4.92 a month was beyond the means of low-income elderly, a significantly higher premium would surely become a financial burden for them. Indeed, such premiums would constitute a financial catastrophe in their own right, outweighing the peace of mind the additional coverage was to provide. Having embraced the principle that all the legislation's costs would be borne by the elderly, Congress had no alternative but to rely on a progressive financing mechanism.

Of course, if the poor would pay less for the new legislation, then those with higher incomes would pay more—possibly a lot more than they would receive in new benefits. This implication was not lost on the architects of the legislation in Congress. Indeed, these lawmakers viewed the legislation in large part as a mechanism for redistributing the Medicare subsidies garnered by the wealthy elderly to those with lower incomes. In the process, most were keenly aware that "the introduction of the ability-to-pay concept" may have constituted "the most far-reaching impact of all of the provisions in the Bill" (U.S. House, Committee on Ways and Means, Subcommittee on Health 1987, 127). The presence of this rationale was repeatedly confirmed in interviews with principals and staff aides on the House Ways and Means Subcommittee on Health and the Senate Finance Committee, as well as other close observers.

For years, many of the lawmakers on these committees had privately been critical of the way in which the nation's social-insurance programs—Social Security and Medicare—provided benefits to the affluent elderly well in excess of such persons' financial contributions to the system and, in the view of many, their financial needs. As this occurred, a significant portion of elderly with incomes just above or below the poverty line faced substantial unmet needs, particularly in the area of health care.

The first step toward retargeting social-insurance benefits away from the wealthiest elderly occurred in 1983, when Congress decided to tax half the value of Social Security benefits for single persons with incomes above $25,000 and for couples with incomes above $32,000 (see Chapter 1). It is significant that this reform was adopted only after considerable controversy as part of an eleventh-hour compromise aimed at saving Social Security from fiscal insolvency. Nevertheless, the event was cited by many of those I interviewed as providing the major precedent for social-insurance policymaking in an era of fiscal scarcity. Indeed, these lawmakers believed that catastrophic-care legislation would build on the 1983 reforms by retargeting social-insurance benefits, not in response to a crisis but as a means of financing proactive social legislation.

If this effort was successful, many foresaw similar principles being applied in the future. Some of those interviewed hoped to use income-targeted premiums to finance a major portion of a federal long-term-care program. ("If this principle had been mastered," said one staffer in a personal interview, "it would have paved the way" for such an effort.) Others viewed the ability-to-pay concept as a possible means of funding deficit-reduction efforts or, more narrowly, ensuring the long-term solvency of the Medicare trust fund. ("Given the long-run financing problems facing the Medicare program in the late 1990s and early 21st century," said health-care expert Gail Wilensky, "this is an important precedent to have established" [U.S. House, Committee on Ways and Means, Subcommittee on Health 1987, 127].)

The major source of dissent with the legislation's financing mechanism arose from senior-citizen interest groups and from supporters in Congress. They argued that imposing all program costs on senior citizens was unfair and constituted "a dangerous departure from the 'social insurance principles' of Medicare" (Pear 1987b). While agreeing that the new benefits should be financed in a deficit-neutral manner and that the elderly should pay something for the benefits, one group—the National Council of Senior Citizens—complained that imposing all the costs on seniors would be overly burdensome to a group that was disproportionately represented among "our most vulnerable citizens" (U.S. House, Committee on Ways and Means, Subcommittee on Health 1987, 164–65). Since 1980, they argued, the elderly had already suffered from "deep cuts" in federal programs serving them.

More significant is that advocates for the elderly worried that the method of financing constituted a "back door" precedent to further "means-testing" within social-insurance programs. In fact, such a mechanism did not constitute a true means-test in which only those with incomes below a certain level are eligible for benefits. Under the catastrophic-care program, all elderly would have access to program benefits regardless of income. Nevertheless, senior-citizen advocates worried that including a visibly progressive financing mechanism in catastrophic care would result in a program that had the characteristics of a means-tested one. Specifically, they feared that this method of financing would sow discontent among affluent seniors who would be compelled to pay amounts well in excess of the benefits they would receive from the new program. When high-income seniors learned that the new program was a bad deal for them personally, they would demand and ultimately win the right to opt out. The result would be a program composed of largely low-income seniors and dependent on general revenues for its survival. In the absence of political pressure by relatively affluent seniors, such a program would take on the characteristics of a welfare program, dependent on the yearly budget process and stigmatizing recipients.

Highly sensitive to the political implications of any proposal tagged with the label "means-test," Representatives Pete Stark and Bill Gradison, chief authors of the House bill, vigilantly protested attempts to use that label to characterize the financing mechanism. "Means-testing has a very bad connotation among the whole social benefits program and I would hope we could find a better word," said Stark. Instead, he and Gradison insisted that the financing mechanism be referred to as a "mandatory user's fee" or an "income-related mandatory user's fee" (Rovner 1987c, 916; U.S. House, Committee on Energy and Commerce Subcommittee 1987, 202). A means-test is an "access limitation," said Stark, making the distinction. "Our proposal does not means test. . . . We relate income but we don't deny access to anybody because they've got too much money" (U.S. House, Committee on Energy and Commerce Subcommittee 1987, 201).

Senior-citizen advocates found Stark and Gradison's distinction semantic. "We have always been opposed to any form of means-testing on the ground that it would push the Medicare program in the direction of welfare," said John Rother, legislative director of AARP (Pear 1987b), "and we always opposed financing the existing package of benefits with income-related premiums."

As an alternative method of financing, AARP, the National Council of Senior Citizens, Villers, and the National Committee to Preserve Social Security and Medicare proposed to pay for various parts of the legislation through an assortment of sources, including increased payroll taxes on workers, tobacco taxes, the extension of Medicare to state and local employees, cost controls on federal health-care programs, and general revenues (U.S. House, Committee on Ways and Means, Subcommittee on Health 1987, 144–85, 548–53). However, with the White House and Congress agreeing that the legislation should be financed solely by the elderly, these revenue sources were not seriously considered.

With the noteworthy exception of the National Committee to Preserve Social Security and Medicare, interest groups representing the elderly ultimately acquiesced to Congress's elderly-only income-related financing, in exchange for inclusion of prescription drugs and other benefits contained in the legislation. Of particular importance was the endorsement of the nation's preeminent senior citizens' group, the 28-million-member American Association of Retired Persons. In agreeing to support the legislation, AARP explicitly endorsed a program that was highly unattractive to its most affluent members, many of whom would pay considerably more in premiums than they received in benefits. Given AARP's commitment to "represent[ing] the interests of all older Americans" and its reputation "as an organization of middle-class to upper-middle-class professionals and executives" (Day 1990, 122), this decision appears difficult to understand.

Two factors help explain the organization's endorsement of the legislation. First and perhaps most important, AARP's politically liberal leadership believed that "the bill's benefits far outweigh[ed] the disadvantages of the financing approach" (*AARP Bulletin,* February 1988). While the prescription-drug benefits were pivotal in the organization's decision to support the catastrophic-care bill, AARP leaders privately were even more enthusiastic about the expanded or new benefits for skilled nursing facilities, home health care, respite care, and spousal impoverishment. These benefits constituted major progress—"Got us half way there," in the words of one high-ranking AARP official interviewed—toward a federally funded long-term-care program. AARP leaders hoped to build on this foundation incrementally in future legislation.[1]

Second, three public-opinion polls conducted on behalf of AARP before passage of the legislation appeared to indicate broad support among the elderly (see Chapter 4). According to an AARP analysis of these data, "the results of these three polls were one of several factors that helped shape AARP's position on benefits and financing for the act" (Straw 1990, 3).

The apparent high degree of public support for legislation believed to constitute good public policy by AARP's leaders made an irrefutable argument for the organization's endorsement.[2] Moreover, the consensus

1. According to this AARP official, once the organization agreed to accept the principle of elderly-only financing in exchange for the added benefits, its support for basing premiums on ability-to-pay principles followed from pragmatic considerations. Otherwise, organization officials believed that many low-income elderly would face excessive financial burdens.
2. Less clear is whether endorsing the legislation served AARP's financial interests. On the one hand, the organization's position as the nation's third-largest originator of Medigap insurance presented it with strong reasons to oppose the legislation (Longman 1989, 16). On the other hand, one of AARP's more profitable activities was as a middleman for the nation's second-largest mail-order drug supply service. With AARP collecting a royalty on every

surrounding the program led AARP officials to believe that there was little need to explain the program to the elderly or to launch any significant effort to build grass-roots support. The organization's leaders saw potential for protest only from the most affluent elderly, who under the legislation would incur personal costs well in excess of benefits. However, they reasoned that this group was small in number, representing no more than 10 to 15 percent of seniors, and therefore could be easily withstood.

While agreement on the principles underlying the legislation's financing occurred quickly, developing the precise mechanism took considerably longer. The matter was not completely resolved until May 1988, when the House-Senate conference reached final agreement on the legislation.

Stark and Gradison originally proposed to finance their version of catastrophic care by taxing the actuarial value of Medicare benefits now financed by the government. In 1988 this would add $1,776 to each Medicare beneficiary's taxable income. But according to Ways and Means staff, 54 percent of beneficiaries would not pay higher taxes because their incomes were too low to affect their tax liability. Stark and Gradison also proposed to finance a portion of the program through a $1.30 monthly premium paid by all beneficiaries.

However, this particular progressive financing mechanism was abandoned under pressure from labor unions and others, who feared it would establish a precedent for taxing fringe benefits such as health insurance (Rovner 1987c, 915–16). In an effort to circumvent the pitfalls of taxing the actuarial value of benefits, Senator Bentsen, in late April 1987, proposed to finance the legislation through a supplemental premium based on the amount of federal taxes paid by beneficiaries. The concept contained the virtues of the Stark-Gradison mechanism without its defects: a majority of the elderly would pay no supplemental premium, but the mechanism set no precedent for taxing fringe benefits. Bentsen's proposal also included a flat premium—$4.00 a month—to be paid by all beneficiaries. Following Bentsen's proposal, Stark and Gradison adopted their own version of the two-premium concept and placed it in their version of the legislation.

Throughout 1987 and the first five months of 1988, members of the House and Senate, separately and then together, devoted considerable energy to fine-tuning the legislation's financing mechanism. Indeed, during this period members of the House Ways and Means Subcommittee on

---

prescription it filled, it stood to gain considerably under the prescription-drug provisions (*Wall Street Journal* 1989 and 1988; see also Califano 1988).

Health and the Senate Finance Committee requested and received frequent estimates detailing how the legislation's distribution of costs would be affected by changes in the financing mechanism or by the inclusion of additional benefits. By virtually all accounts of those interviewed, members of these committees developed a deep awareness of the degree to which the legislation redistributed costs from low-income elderly to high-income elderly.

The final legislation included a highly progressive financing mechanism to fund the new benefits. Two-thirds of program costs were to be funded by the supplemental premium on beneficiaries with tax liabilities. In 1989 this surtax was set at 15 percent of one's tax liability (for those with $150 or more of federal income taxes) up to a maximum of $800 for individuals, $1,600 for couples. By 1993 the surtax would rise to 28 percent and the maximum payment to $1,050 for individuals, $2,100 for couples. The remaining one-third of new costs would be paid for by a new $4.00 monthly premium levied on all Medicare recipients. The premium would rise gradually to $10.50 a month by 1993.

According to the Congressional Budget Office (1988b, 8), only 36 percent of Medicare recipients would pay any surtax in 1989, while only 5 percent would be liable for the maximum premium. Price Waterhouse, in 1989, calculated that a single person with an income of $20,000 and a married couple with an income of $30,000 would each owe approximately $158 in supplemental premiums. The maximum surtax would take effect at $45,000 for singles and at $75,000 for couples (U.S. Senate, Committee on Finance 1990, 104–5).

Further, for many seniors the costs of the legislation would be compounded by the fact that approximately 20 percent of all Medicare enrollees had part or all of their Medigap premium costs paid by former employers (Congressional Budget Office 1988b, 12). Although the legislation contained provisions requiring employers to provide additional benefits or refunds equal to the actuarial value of the duplicated benefits, the compensation was due only for a brief transitional period, after which employers would likely curtail such coverage or rebates. Thus, under the program this group of senior citizens would effectively "pay twice," losing benefits they had been receiving as part of their compensation package from employers, and paying to receive benefits.

The financing system contained in the Medicare Catastrophic Coverage Act (MCCA) marked a precedent in social-insurance policy-making. As Table 3.1 shows, in contrast to Social Security and Medicare, the passage

Table 3.1. The evolution of social insurance in the United States

	OASI (Social Security)	HI (Medicare A)	SMI (Medicare B)	MCCA
Percentage of program funded by current recipients	Trivial[a]	Trivial[a]	25%	100%
Overt redistribution of $ occurring within cohorts of elderly	No	No	No	Yes
Progressive benefit-cost relationship among recipients (poor receive higher return than the wealthy)	Yes[b]	Yes[b]	No—All pay same premiums	Yes
A good buy for all recipients (benefits on average are greater than costs [taxes + premiums])	Yes[c]	Yes[d]	Yes	No

[a]Although earnings of those over age 65 are subject to FICA taxes, relatively few such persons work. In 1992 the labor-force participation rate for elderly men and women was 16.1 percent and 8.3 percent respectively. Furthermore, among those elderly who work, part-time employment is prevalent. (U.S. House, Committee on Ways and Means 1993, 272.)

[b]The formulas for calculating OASI benefits give those who contribute relatively low amounts in FICA taxes a larger ratio of benefits to costs than those who contribute higher amounts. In addition, all recipients receive the same Medicare A coverage regardless of their level of FICA contributions.

[c]Heretofore, all contributors, on average, have received benefits in excess of the value of payments to the system. As a result of the 1983 reforms, only future recipients with relatively low incomes are assured of a positive benefit-contribution ratio.

[d]According to a 1988 study, during the first twenty years of Medicare's existence (1966–85), retirees, on average, paid taxes equivalent to only 5 percent of the value of the benefits they received (Vogel 1988, 82; see also U.S. House, Committee on Ways and Means 1993, 1301–4; and Congressional Budget Office 1989).

of the MCCA marked the first social-insurance program expansion to be financed completely by beneficiaries themselves and to engage in easily seen income-redistribution among them. And while the legislation maintained a progressive benefit-payroll tax relationship that allowed low-income participants to receive higher rates of return on contributions, the new system departed from the previously unstated but closely adhered to principle that participation should be financially worthwhile for all recipients. For the first time in the history of U.S. social-insurance policy-making, significant numbers of participants—in this case the approximately 30 percent of the elderly with the highest incomes—would be worse off through participation in the new program.

In an attempt to design the legislation in a fiscally responsible manner, the architects took the additional step of "front-loading" the catastrophic-care program so that premiums were to be collected before the benefits became available. This was done "in order to build up financial reserves in the event costs exceeded initial estimates" (Rovner 1989l, 2715). Consequently, under the final legislation, benefits for hospital stays and skilled nursing facilities would go into effect in 1989, but coverage for physician charges, mammograms, and respite care would be unavailable until 1990, while the prescription-drug benefit was not to be phased in fully until 1993. With the program's flat premium due beginning January 1989 and the supplemental premium to be collected starting that tax year, many seniors would incur significant costs before receiving any coverage, much less actual benefits, from the legislation. Thus, in the program's first year new premiums would average $145, well in excess of the $62 value of the new benefits. Only in 1993, when the entire program was in place, would the value of new benefits ($322) approach average new premiums ($331) (Tolchin 1989c).

Although not apparent until later, the fiscally responsible decision to "front-load" the legislation's costs, like the decision to impose the full burden of its financing on the elderly, would emerge as a key obstacle to public support for the program.

4

PASSAGE OF THE MCCA

During 1987 and 1988 the House and Senate each voted twice by substantial margins to approve the legislation that became the Medicare Catastrophic Coverage Act of 1988. In July 1987 the House passed its version by a vote of 302 to 127. Eleven months later the conference report containing the final version passed by a wider margin (328 to 72). The Senate voted to support both its version and the conference report by identical 86-to-11 votes.

In light of the degree of redistribution present in the legislation, it does not appear that these high levels of congressional support can be explained easily. Lowi (1964), whose "arenas of power" scheme first identified redistributive policy-making as a distinct type of politics, notes that issues involving redistribution "cut closer than any others [distributive, regulatory, etc.] along class lines and activate interests in what are roughly class terms." In addition, the MCCA appears to be an example of what Wilson (1992, 436) has termed *entrepreneurial politics*, where "society as a whole or some large part of it benefits from a policy that imposes substantial costs on some small identifiable segment of society." In such cases, the affected minority is likely to exhibit intense opposition to the legislation. By contrast, "the large group of prospective beneficiaries may be unconvinced of the benefit or regard it as too small to be worth fighting for." Wilson further notes, "It is remarkable that policies of this sort are ever adopted."[1]

1. Wilson himself (1992, 489) views the MCCA as an example of majoritarian politics where "policies promise benefits to large numbers of people at a cost that large numbers of people will have to bear" (433). His perspective is understandable, given the efforts of advocates to depict the legislation in this manner (indeed, this is a central point of this

Still others have made the related observation that "controversy character-izes redistributive policy because it attempts to reallocate items and symbols of value among different groups in society" (Ripley and Franklin 1984, 168).

Given the apparently problematic nature of redistributive policy-making, why did so many in Congress vote for the legislation? In explaining this phenomenon, we shall also explore a closely related issue: the degree to which rank-and-file members of Congress were aware of the financing mechanism, particularly the supplemental premium, and understood its political implications.

The conclusions are twofold. First, while discussion of the financing did not monopolize the deliberations over catastrophic care, the issue was addressed frequently and in enough detail by fellow members during floor debates and through the efforts of one key interest group—the National Committee to Preserve Social Security and Medicare—that rank-and-file members were certainly aware of its presence and implications. Second, even though they were undoubtedly aware that there could be controversy over how the program would be financed, rank-and-file members opted to approve the legislation because the political environment was almost en-tirely favorable to passage. Three factors were particularly influential: (1) the presence of the Pepper bill, which rank-and-file members could avert by embracing the MCCA; (2) the endorsement of the MCCA by congressional elites, President Reagan, and, perhaps most significant, the American Asso-ciation of Retired Persons; and (3) public-opinion surveys from the period that appeared to show widespread support among the elderly. Media coverage of the development and passage of the MCCA during 1987 and the first half of 1988 may be responsible for the initially favorable view seniors had. During that period the major print and electronic media generally failed to provide more than cursory mention of the most contro-versial aspect—the method of financing. While the monthly *AARP Bulletin* addressed this aspect more critically and in greater detail than the objective media, the issue was discussed in the context of stories that largely reflected the organization's favorable view of the legislation.

Each vote in Congress to approve the MCCA was preceded by extensive

chapter and of the study in general). However, the entrepreneurial-politics construct better characterizes the MCCA because a large proportion of the program's costs (more than 80 percent) were to be imposed on a minority of the elderly (the most affluent 40 percent), who would be liable for the supplemental premium.

floor debate.[2] On these occasions, three aspects of the legislation—its benefits, its costs, and the method of financing—emerged as key areas of disagreement. These issues remained controversial following passage, and indeed foreshadowed the disputes that would later engulf the program.

The first area of disagreement concerned the relative importance of the legislation's benefits. Opponents of the MCCA argued that characterizing the act as "catastrophic care" was a misnomer because it failed to address "the true catastrophic health problem" confronting America's senior citizens—namely, long-term care (U.S. Congress 1987, H6464; see also U.S. Congress 1988, H3871, S15177; 1987, H6471, H6483, H6488). They argued that the legislation provided coverage for expenses that were not truly catastrophic to most elderly. In their view, this was particularly true of the MCCA prescription-drug benefit. "Although $600 in annual drug bills—for example—can create problems in many cases," said Senator Nancy Kassebaum, "this is not the concern that tens of thousands of dollars in nursing home care represent. This is where our efforts should be directed" (U.S. Congress 1987, S15178). Opponents also pointed out that more than 70 percent of the elderly held Medigap policies covering many of the benefits the MCCA included (U.S. Congress 1988, S7387, S7405; 1987, H6488, S15144).

Supporters of the MCCA countered these criticisms by touting the importance of the program's benefits, particularly its prescription-drug provisions. They noted that few Medigap policies offered coverage for drug expenses and that such costs constituted the elderly's second-largest source of out-of-pocket expenses behind long-term care. With respect to the legislation's failure to include coverage for long-term care, MCCA advocates agreed that this was a significant deficiency but argued that such a goal was unattainable given the financing constraints of the period (U.S. Congress 1988, S7259; 1987, H6469, S15021). At the same time, a number of the supporters argued that the new and expanded benefits for skilled nursing facilities, respite care, and spousal impoverishment constituted significant progress toward comprehensive federal coverage of long-term care. Indeed, MCCA supporters viewed the legislation not as an end in itself but as something to be elaborated on in future years (U.S. Congress 1988, H3858; 1987, H6475).

Second, supporters and opponents disagreed about whether program

2. See U.S. Congress 1988, H3854–89, S7257–67, S7386–414; 1987, H6461–545, S14090–105, S15021–23, S15086–183.

revenues would be sufficient to cover benefit costs. Opponents feared that the costs of the benefits, particularly prescription drugs, would escalate rapidly and outstrip the ability or willingness of senior citizens to pay for them.[3] When this occurred, they feared that "elderly groups" would "come to Congress seeking a cut in premiums" (U.S. Congress 1987, H6462–63; see also U.S. Congress 1987, S15145). At this point, said Senator Steven Symms, "There will . . . be considerable pressure to raise revenues from any source—payroll taxes, general revenues, excise taxes—to pay for benefits. When that occurs, the hope [that] this problem would remain self-financing and budget neutral would fade away" (U.S. Congress 1987, S15105; see also U.S. Congress 1988, S7388; 1987, H6483, H6489, H6492, S15177; Pear 1987d). As a precedent for this scenario, opponents cited the early history of the Hospital Insurance portion of the Medicare program when Congress dealt with the problem of rapidly increasing costs by raising payroll taxes on workers (U.S. Congress 1987, S15097).

Advocates responded to these criticisms by asserting variously that the legislation was "deficit neutral" (U.S. Congress 1988, H3873, S7262), "revenue neutral" (U.S. Congress 1987, H6486), "fiscally responsible" (U.S. Congress 1987, H6478), and "would not cost the treasury one red cent" (U.S. Congress 1987, H6463). In support of these claims, Senator Lloyd Bentsen noted that concerns over costs were behind the decision to phase in the prescription-drug benefit over three years (U.S. Congress 1988, S7258). In the House, Representative Pete Stark referred to "cost control

---

3. One particularly contentious subissue related to the program's costs concerned the degree to which AIDS patients would benefit from its prescription-drug provisions. Under Social Security regulations, AIDS patients who had paid into the system qualified for Social Security disability benefits regardless of age after a five-month waiting period, and twenty-four months later became eligible for Medicare. The prospect of saddling senior citizens with the potentially explosive costs of such drug therapy alarmed a number of conservative House Republicans (Rovner 1987h, 1638–39). Because the legislation was to be financed solely by the elderly, they charged that senior citizens were being unfairly singled out "to shoulder the burden for an exploding population of AIDS victims." House Democrats, led by Henry Waxman, countered that this argument was "a straw man" because nearly all AIDS patients died within a year of being diagnosed and consequently never qualified for benefits. Even if life spans of AIDS patients were to increase so that many qualified for Medicare, Waxman pointed out, the federal government was hurrying to develop less-expensive alternatives to AZT that could well be available by that time. Not persuaded by such arguments, Representative Phillip Crane offered an amendment during the 1987 House debate to return the legislation to committee with instructions "to ascertain or determine the additional payments required of senior citizens" resulting from drug payments to AIDS patients. Although the motion was rejected 244 to 187, House Republicans continued to invoke the issue in later debates (see U.S. Congress 1988, H3860, H3867, H3880).

measures" in the legislation, limiting payments to pharmacies and encouraging the use of low-cost generic drugs (U.S. Congress 1987, H3887). Also, advocates cited studies of the Congressional Budget Office and the Joint Committee on Taxation that projected revenues would exceed program costs during the program's early years (U.S. Congress 1988, S7260).

This issue was a sensitive one for program advocates. The *Congressional Quarterly* reported that, during the 1987 Senate debate, "both Democratic and Republican sponsors were visibly agitated at the accusation that the measure was not, or would not, continue to be self-financing" (Rovner 1987i, 2678). In the House, "some Democrats said privately that they were uncomfortable with the uncertainty about the new benefits' costs" (Rovner 1987h, 1637), while Ways and Means Chairman Dan Rostenkowski, a major supporter of the legislation, admitted being "concerned" about the costs of the prescription-drug benefit (U.S. Congress 1987, H6462).[4] Even Representative Bill Gradison initially opted to support a less-expensive Republican substitute instead of the legislation bearing his name, in the belief that the elderly would ultimately "balk" at the latter's "ever increasing costs" (U.S. Congress 1987, H6464).

Finally, the financing mechanism of the MCCA, particularly its system of income-related premiums, engendered considerable controversy. During the debates, the majority of those who spoke or placed statements in the *Congressional Record* addressed the issue. In the process, specific facts concerning the distribution of costs and how much one would owe in supplemental and flat premiums at particular income levels were widely circulated among members of Congress. More important, examination of the floor debates reveals that many legislators had firm beliefs concerning the financing of social-insurance programs and that there was no consensus on the issue.

Predictably, the MCCA's architects and staunchest supporters were also the strongest advocates of its method of financing. They both defended the financing as a necessary requirement for passage and argued that it was a fair and equitable policy that would establish an important precedent for future social-insurance policy-making.

During the debates, advocates openly acknowledged both the intent

---

4. Rovner (1987h, 1637) reports that these House Democrats voted to support the legislation "in the hope that a less ambitious alternative could be worked out in a House-Senate conference." However, although the final version of the legislation differed from the House and Senate bills on a number of details, the general scope of its benefits remained largely unchanged.

underlying the financing mechanism and the implications for future legislation. According to Representative Sander Levin, inclusion of the income-related premium demonstrated "that we can redistribute the financing of reforms more fairly, so that those with greater incomes can help ease the burden on others who are less well off" (U.S. Congress 1988, H3871). Representative Gradison was more blunt, saying of the legislation's progressive financing: "Elderly Americans with the ability to pay more should contribute more to sustain Medicare" (U.S. Congress 1987, H6464). Senator David Durenberger underlined the extent to which MCCA's financing marked a departure from previous social-insurance programs: "For the first time in the history of the program the financing of Medicare will not be solely on the backs of workers in the form of the payroll tax or the beneficiaries in a flat, across the board assessment. Rather over 60 percent of the final costs will be supported by the 40 percent of higher income Medicare beneficiaries." The result of this, he said, was that "low and moderate income elderly and disabled will gain the most overall from these new benefits and will have to pay the least" (U.S. Congress 1988, S7400).

The logical implication of these statements was that many relatively wealthy elderly were likely to receive considerably less in benefits from the MCCA program than they would pay in flat and supplemental premiums. It is important, however, to note that congressional advocates of the MCCA refused to acknowledge explicitly the redistributive implications of the program, probably because they were afraid of the political consequences of such an admission. Instead, they admitted only that the legislation would mean a slight "dilution" of the Medicare subsidies received by the wealthiest elderly (U.S. Congress 1987, S15110). Advocates were quick to note that, even including the MCCA, "no one" among the elderly would "be asked to pay more than the actuarial value of the [Medicare A and B] subsidy they themselves receive" (U.S. Congress 1988, H3858). Thus, in Representative Gradison's words, "Even if they [the wealthiest elderly] are asked to foot more of the bill [for MCCA]" Medicare would "still be a great insurance deal" (U.S. Congress 1987, H6464).

Advocates also emphasized that the program's effect on well-to-do seniors would be mitigated by reductions in the cost of Medigap policies purchased by more than 70 percent of the elderly. "The idea that [the MCCA is] going to be expensive is correct but what most seniors are carrying around is even more expensive," said Representative Stark (Bluestein 1988). Under the MCCA program, private insurers were mandated to revise their policies so there would be no duplication of the benefits offered by the new program. Although vague as to the exact magnitude of such savings, the legislation's proponents argued that after the program was put into effect the cost of Medigap policies would decrease (U.S. Congress 1988, H3866; S7395).[5] Indeed, a number of legislators speculated, no doubt hopefully, that the MCCA would ultimately cause the Medigap market to wither away, as seniors declined to purchase coverage for Medicare's remaining deductibles and co-payments (U.S. Congress 1988, H3887; 1987, H6501).

Some of the legislation's strongest supporters viewed the financing structure as establishing an important precedent for future government programs. Senator George Mitchell, for example, termed the MCCA, and particularly its income-related method of financing, "a historic step" and predicted that it would "be viewed as one of the major turning points in American social policy" (U.S. Congress 1988, S7265). In the House, Representative Gradison believed that the financing pointed the way "for Congressional action in the future to deal with the remaining gaps in health protection for our citizens—young and old alike" (U.S. Congress 1988, H3858). Likewise, Representative Levin predicted: "Our progress in these financing areas will help us as we turn to other health care needs including long-term care" (U.S. Congress 1988, H3871).

The legislation's method of financing was unpopular with opponents of the program, and even with a number of supporters. Critics denounced the supplemental premium alternately as "financially burdensome" (U.S. Congress 1987, H6465), "an incredible tax increase" (1987, H6472), "a massive tax increase" (1987, H6479), "a catastrophic disaster for America's senior citizens" (1987, H6488), "a financial catastrophe for senior citizens" (1987, H6487), and "a whopping new tax on the elderly" (1988, H3883).

While most criticisms made no explicit reference to the redistributive effects of the supplemental premium, a number of legislators addressed that issue. For example, Senator Don Nickles, the Senate's most outspoken opponent of the legislation, referred to the supplemental premium as "an income redistribution scheme" where those with higher incomes were going to pay more for an identical set of benefits (U.S. Congress 1987, S15095). In the House, Representative Bill Frenzel noted that the legislation created

5. AARP concurred with this assessment. In the words of one organization official, "Since private insurance plans will be insuring less risk, you should see a price reduction in current policies. . . . Or you should see new policies that hold their prices steady and offer coverage in new areas" (*AARP Bulletin* 1987c).

"a mandatory surtax, the so-called supplemental premium which adds a new tax to middle and upper income elderly bearing no relationship to benefits received" (U.S. Congress 1988, H3871).

Although less caustic, a number of MCCA supporters also expressed reservations about its method of financing. In the House, Representative Don Bonker worried that the system of supplemental premiums "puts too much of the burden directly on beneficiaries," while Representative Mario Biaggi termed the surtax "unfair as it pertains to the elderly with income in the lower [tax] bracket" (U.S. Congress 1988, H3880, H3883). In the Senate, one particularly reluctant supporter, Senator Pete Domenici, called the legislation's financing "a huge tax increase" on older Americans and worried that it would prove "unsustainable" (U.S. Congress 1988, S7392).

Critics of the financing also disagreed with the contention that it established a precedent for funding future government programs. Indeed, many believed just the opposite—that the MCCA utilized "an important source of funding: higher premiums that perhaps really ought to be saved for the purpose of paying for the more necessary, and more expensive, benefits of long-term care" (U.S. Congress 1988, S7396). "It is difficult to imagine our asking the elderly to pay the $42.60 per month premiums required five years from now under this bill," explained Representative Anthony Beilenson (U.S. Congress 1988, H3884; see also Beilenson 1988). "It is inconceivable that we will ask them to pay even more than that, even for the most sought-after benefit."

Rank-and-file congressmen also became aware of the MCCA's shortcomings through the efforts of the National Committee to Preserve Social Security and Medicare. Founded in 1982 with the self-professed mission of "saving" Social Security benefits for senior citizens, the 4.5-million-member organization was the only age-based interest group to oppose the legislation. Its objections had to do with the program's failure to cover long-term care and with its elderly-only method of financing.

The National Committee was particularly outspoken with respect to the latter issue. From its perspective, "this financing limitation" ignored "the fact that the problem of catastrophic health care costs for seniors is not generationally neutral." "By the time of retirement," the National Committee asserted, "[elderly] individuals no longer have resources to finance all of their health care" (U.S. House, Committee on Ways and Means, Subcommittee on Health 1987, 551–52). Thus, it reasoned, "to expect seniors to pay the full cost of health care will not solve the problem of catastrophic illness, but will continue to foster the problem." As an alternative, the National Committee urged that the burden of financing be shared by younger generations, who, it argued, were better able to assume such costs. This arrangement, it reminded, "is the overall principle for current Medicare financing."

Before the debates over the MCCA, the National Committee to Preserve Social Security and Medicare was "well known but hardly well-loved on Capitol Hill" (Rovner 1988a, 777; see also Rovner 1988b, 778–79). Named one of the nation's worst public-interest groups in the March 1988 issue of *Washington Monthly*, the organization had a reputation for adopting militant, uncompromising stands on policy issues and using "misleading" and "inflammatory" methods in its fund-raising and political-action efforts. One example of the National Committee's activities involved a January 1983 solicitation from its founder and president, James Roosevelt (a former congressman and oldest son of President Franklin D. Roosevelt), urging senior citizens to "act to save Social Security and Medicare." Sent in official-looking envelopes urging immediate attention to the "time-dated legal documents" inside, the letters set off a barrage of telephone calls and mail to congressmen "from frightened, confused constituents who wanted to know how the Social Security system could be in trouble again so soon after it apparently had been shored up" (Rovner 1988b, 778).

In many respects, the National Committee's tactics in opposing the MCCA paralleled those of this earlier incident. Although the organization's activities gained notoriety only after the MCCA became law in June 1988 (see Chapter 6), the National Committee did actively attempt to scuttle the program before the act was passed. The first of these efforts occurred in August 1987, following the House vote approving the legislation. In the National Committee's newsletter *Saving Social Security* (National Committee 1987), Executive Director Landis Neal stated that the organization would "pull out all stops to win changes in the legislation in the Senate." During September 1987 it mailed letters to more than 1.5 million senior citizens warning that the bill's supplemental premiums would bring "huge increases in your Medicare costs" (Rich 1987b).

The National Committee's first appeal on catastrophic care (as well as subsequent appeals) brought an immediate response from substantial numbers of senior citizens. On September 14 the *Washington Post* reported that senators were "receiving a surge of constituency mail questioning the premiums" (Rich 1987b). Ken Hoagland, a spokesman for the National Committee, estimated that during the next few weeks senators were likely to receive 70,000 to 80,000 letters from organization members. The same article also reported that members of Congress heard complaints "about the financing of the package generally" during recent trips home.

Following Senate passage of the legislation in October 1987, the National Committee continued its efforts to thwart the measure by attempting to defeat the House-Senate conference agreement in a floor vote. In March 1988 the National Committee announced that a "Legislative Alert" had been mailed to all its members "in the hope that hundreds of thousands of letters would cause members to vote down the conferees' recommended bill" (National Committee 1988a).

Later that month, on March 31, the National Committee (1988) took the additional step of placing an advertisement in the *Washington Post* attacking the legislation. Under the introduction "A Message to Congress," followed by a large bold-type proclamation reading "Seniors Won't Thank You," the National Committee issued the following warning:

> A vote for the so-called catastrophic care legislation now pending is a vote you'll regret this November. For limited improvements in health care coverage under Medicare, premiums will jump for nearly every senior citizen. . . .
>
> Political leaders who think that seniors will thank them for this flawed and expensive piece of legislation are deluding themselves. Those who believe that passing this bill would be a good "first step" toward true catastrophic care relief are mistaken. Passage of H.R. 2470 would be a step in the wrong direction towards 100% financing of Medicare programs by the elderly.
>
> Don't make a mistake that will harm and anger your senior constituents. Vote against the pending catastrophic care legislation.

The National Committee's campaign against the MCCA gave many members of Congress second thoughts. A March 26 *Congressional Quarterly* article entitled "Catastrophic-Costs Conferees Irked by Lobbying Assaults" reported that "all members of Congress are being flooded with mail prompted by the Roosevelt group" (Rovner 1988a, 777). Advocates of the legislation admitted that such efforts had caused "some heartburn" and "skittishness" among rank-and-file members, although they generally described "the campaigns against MCCA as more of an irritant than an impediment to the bill's enactment" (Rovner 1988a, 777). While the last statement proved true, the National Committee's campaign to stop the legislation remained a continuing source of discomfort for MCCA supporters. As late as May 1988, less than one month before the final votes on the conference agreement, the *Congressional Quarterly* reported that "conferees in both chambers" were responding "heatedly to reports that other members' mail is running against the bill" (Rovner 1988d, 1290).

In spite of all the concerns raised about the MCCA, particularly its financing, by the National Committee, congressional opponents, and even a number of supporters, overwhelming majorities in the House and Senate twice voted to approve the legislation. While many in Congress might have harbored doubts about MCCA, a number of factors combined to assuage them.

The first of these concerned the Pepper bill. Just as Representative Claude Pepper had used his legislation as a prod to expand MCCA benefits in early 1987 (see Chapter 2), his continuing efforts on its behalf through June 1988 gave rank-and-file congressmen an incentive to support the legislation. During the period when Congress considered the legislation, Pepper and his supporters lobbied hard for his bill, H.R. 3436, which sought to provide a federal benefit for long-term home health care. While many House members were sympathetic to this objective, they also expressed misgivings about the general lack of cost controls, the method of financing, and the procedures used to bring it to the House floor (see Chapter 2). Nevertheless, Pepper's influence on issues concerning the elderly was unparalleled, and significant numbers of House Democrats were politically indebted to him.[6] Under normal circumstances, many might have lacked the will to oppose him. Fortunately for these legislators, the presence of the MCCA, a bill perceived to be moderate in scope and more fiscally responsible than Pepper's, offered a way out of this dilemma. By voting for the MCCA, many congressmen were able to resist the Pepper bill without appearing to vote against the political interests of the elderly.

Second, rank-and-file congressmen were undoubtedly influenced by the broad and influential coalition supporting the MCCA. Within the federal government, the legislation was supported by a wide range of powerful elected officials. In the House, the legislation was enthusiastically endorsed by Speaker Jim Wright, who had supported inclusion of the prescription-drug benefit as a means of putting a Democratic stamp on the legislation

---

6. For example, in 1982 Pepper had made political appearances for seventy Democratic candidates in twenty-five states (Rovner 1988g, 1605).

(see Chapter 2). In addition, influential committee chairmen Dan Rostenkowski of Ways and Means and John Dingell of Energy and Commerce
placed their considerable influence behind the measure. Finally, Gradison's
ultimate endorsement of the legislation bearing his name (following the
defeat of a less-expensive Republican substitute) provided the bill with the
trappings of bipartisan support.

In the Senate, support for the legislation was truly bipartisan, with
Democrats Bentsen and Mitchell and Republicans Heinz, Durenberger,
Dole, and Chafee playing key roles in crafting and speaking on behalf of
the legislation. The Reagan administration's September 1987 endorsement
of the MCCA was also probably influential in shoring up support for
the legislation among wavering moderate Republicans and Democrats in
both chambers.

The most important stamp of approval came from the American Association of Retired Persons. During the period when Congress considered
the legislation, the 28-million-member organization enjoyed the virtually
unquestioned reputation as foremost representative of the nation's senior
citizens. Many in Congress appeared to assume—incorrectly as events
would later reveal—that AARP closely consulted its rank-and-file members
on political issues, reflected their views, and was capable of easily mobilizing them on behalf of such positions.

AARP's crucial role as the preeminent group backing the legislation is
indisputable. In addition to playing a significant role in expanding the
benefits provided by the MCCA (see Chapter 2), the organization lobbied
rank-and-file congressmen intensively to support the measure. Among those
I interviewed, virtually all described AARP's efforts as highly influential in
garnering such support. During floor debates over the legislation, supporters in both chambers cited AARP's endorsement as evidence that the bill
enjoyed broad support among the elderly (U.S. Congress 1988, H3887,
H3888, S7410). Even when the legislation was under attack from the
National Committee and the Pharmaceutical Manufacturers Association
(which feared that the legislation's prescription-drug provisions would lead
to cost controls on pharmaceuticals) during March 1988, Representative
Henry Waxman confidently stated: "As long as the AARP and National
Council of Senior Citizens continues to support it, I think Congress will
too" (Rovner 1988a, 780).

Finally, rank-and-file congressmen may have been influenced by public
opinion.[7] Despite the efforts of the National Committee, surveys of senior

7. Although there is considerable research on the relationship of politics to public opinion,

citizens conducted under the auspices of AARP during 1987 and early 1988 appeared to reveal strong overall support for the legislation and the specific benefits it contained (Straw 1990, 3–7). And during that period, support for the legislation among the elderly rose from 78 percent in April 1987 to 91 percent in May 1988, and support for specific items, such as increased coverage of acute hospital stays, physician costs, and prescription drugs, had similar high levels. Such findings allowed supporters in Congress to dismiss the negative feedback received by many in Congress as representative of only a small minority of relatively wealthy elderly who would pay the surtax, or of lower-income elderly who misunderstood the legislation's financing.

However, the early AARP surveys appear to have measured what Yankelovich (1991, 42) has termed "mass opinion" (e.g., "poor quality public opinion") rather than "public judgment" defined as "good quality public opinion in the sense of opinion that is stable, consistent and responsible." For example, in the surveys, preferences concerning the MCCA were expressed in response to questions that made only vague reference to the financing provisions. Although the second and third AARP surveys did note that two new premiums would finance these benefits—"one levied on all Medicare enrollees, and the other (an income related premium) levied on enrollees with annual incomes above $10,000"—such statements avoided the controversial term "surtax" while providing little information on the specific costs Medicare recipients would pay under the program. Thus, by deemphasizing the financing provisions, the AARP surveys failed to confront those surveyed with difficult trade-offs that forced them to face the consequences of their views. As a result, their true opinions about the legislation were poorly measured.

Indeed, the negative response of the elderly to questions dealing solely with the legislation's "elderly only" method of financing serves to underline this point. Asked to choose among a number of financing options in the April 1987 survey, only 5 percent of the elderly expressed support for "additional taxes of elderly taxpayers *only*" (emphasis added). Also notably lacking in the same survey was support for the option of funding the program through "additional premiums paid by Medicare beneficiaries,"

---

few studies have employed public opinion as a variable influencing public policy (Niemi 1983; Margolis and Mauser 1989, 2–3). It is difficult, if not impossible, to document specific instances where public opinion was enough to determine a specific policy outcome. Nevertheless, public opinion may play a significant if not easily detectable role in public-policy outcomes. For one thing, public officials might adopt positions by attempting to anticipate public preferences before they are fully formed or articulated (Arnold 1990).

with only 26 percent of the elderly in favor. The two succeeding AARP surveys, undertaken in September 1987 and May 1988, pursued these issues by asking respondents how they felt "about requiring Medicare beneficiaries to pay for all of the new benefits." While the percentage of seniors favoring such a proposal declined from 36 percent to 30 percent during this period, opposition was substantial and increased from 54 percent to 66 percent (Straw 1990, 7). However, with the preponderance of survey evidence suggesting that senior citizens overwhelmingly supported the legislation, the implications of these responses seem to have been overlooked, ignored, or held in abeyance by AARP and congressional supporters.

Media coverage of the development and passage of the MCCA may account for the generally favorable early assessments.[8] An examination of the reporting on the MCCA by the print and electronic media before the legislation was passed reveals that the most controversial aspect of the legislation—its method of financing (particularly the system of supplemental premiums)—received little attention and even less critical analysis.

Between January 1987 and June 1988, the *New York Times*, the *Washington Post*, and the *Wall Street Journal* frequently mentioned the basic facts of the financing mechanism, including the two-tiered system of premiums and the $800 maximum supplemental premium. However, the subject was usually part of a considerably longer discussion of the many benefits contained in the legislation. In addition, the stories generally neglected to mention the degree to which the legislation's financing constituted a departure from past financing of social-insurance programs—for example, that the MCCA would be the first piece of social-insurance legislation to be financed solely by the elderly and to base premiums on ability to pay. Moreover, with only a few exceptions, reports failed to provide any indication that the method of financing might be unpopular with a significant segment of the elderly. Almost none of the writers even attempted to ask average senior citizens about any aspect of the legislation. Virtually everyone quoted was either an academic expert or a government official.[9]

8. Although there is little research on such matters, a number of studies indicate that the media might play a highly influential role in the formation of public opinion (Iyengar and Kinder 1987; Page et al. 1987). In addition, decision-makers, aware of the media's influence, may pursue policies in response to or in anticipation of news coverage on public opinion (Linsky 1986).

9. A more systematic analysis of print media coverage preceding passage independently confirms virtually all the findings set forth in this paragraph. See Fan and Norem 1992.

Exceptions to this general pattern of reporting did exist. The *Washington Post* (Rich 1987d) and the *New York Times* (Pear 1987b) each ran one article that explored the legislation's financing in significant detail. These newspapers and the *Wall Street Journal* also mentioned the financing as a major reason for supporting (as did the *Times* [1988] and the *Post* [1987]) or opposing the legislation (as did the *Journal* [1988]). A number of op-ed pieces highly critical of the financing also appeared in these newspapers (Beilenson 1988; Ferrara 1988). Taken together, however, these examples constituted only a small portion of what major newspapers printed about the legislation before passage.

If the degree of attention the print media paid to the MCCA's financing was merely inadequate, then the electronic media's discussion of the topic was virtually nonexistent during this period. Reporting on the legislation itself was actually infrequent. Between November 1986 and June 1988, nightly news on the three major commercial networks broadcast only seventeen stories where the legislation was the main topic—less than one a month.[10] And the vast majority of these stories—fourteen—were aired before mid-March 1987 and concerned the Reagan administration's deliberations over whether to accept the Bowen plan and subsequent criticism of its proposal. Of the three remaining stories (two on NBC, one on CBS), one mentioned some basic facts of the legislation's financing—that it would be financed by the elderly themselves through premiums of up to $800 yearly (NBC, June 2, 1988)—while another included the only mention of criticism of the surtax that appeared before the legislation was passed: Representative William Dannemeyer, on the House floor, complaining that the program would impose steep taxes on the elderly (CBS, June 2, 1988).

The failure of the media to emphasize the financing was probably the result of a number of factors. Certainly the sheer complexity of the legislation crowded out detailed discussions of the issue. This may have been particularly true in the case of television news coverage, where severe constraints exist with respect to time. Reporters covering the story may also have been influenced by the generally favorable political environment surrounding it. It bears repeating that, with the exception of the National Committee to Preserve Social Security and Medicare, virtually every influential political force, including AARP, supported the legislation. These

10. For this analysis, "stories" are defined as taped reports by correspondents over twenty seconds in length that were concerned solely or mainly with the legislation. Tapes of these stories were obtained from the Vanderbilt Television News Archives.

factors, combined with the previously discussed efforts of congressional architects to downplay the redistributive implications of the financing, probably left reporters unalert to the controversies that might surround the program. As a result, the vast majority of senior citizens were not aware of important aspects of the legislation, particularly those concerning its costs to them.

In contrast to the major print and electronic media, the financing was addressed in considerably more depth in the *AARP Bulletin*, sent monthly to the organization's 28 million members. As the legislation passed Congress, articles mentioned important details of the financing—including who was liable for the supplemental premium, and estimates of premium liabilities at certain income levels (1987c). Of equal importance, coverage emphasized the precedent-setting nature of the financing, explaining on numerous occasions that the elderly would pay all of the costs and that the supplemental premium was progressively structured (see especially *AARP Bulletin* 1988).

Indeed, the articles emphasized AARP's opposition to these principles and the legislation's method of financing in general. Organization officials were quoted as saying that elderly-only financing was "unfair" and that "older Americans should pay part of the bill but not *all* of it" (1987c); progressively structured premiums were referred to as a possible " 'back door' form of means-testing" on Medicare (1987c); and finally, references to the financing mechanism were frequently followed or preceded by the words "far from perfect" (1988, 1987a, 1987b) or "flawed" (1987c). A December 1987 article even included a pledge by AARP's John Rother "to work to broaden the financial base of this legislation" (1987d), even though the organization had previously compromised this principle in exchange for inclusion of the prescription-drug benefit.

In spite of its generally critical reporting of MCCA's financing, however, the *AARP Bulletin* presented the information in a context that was favorable to the legislation. In fact, its coverage largely reflected the assessment of a key executive of the organization in the February 1988 issue, that "the bill's benefits far outweigh the disadvantages of the financing approach." Thus, discussions of the financing were more than balanced by detailed explanations of its numerous benefits. More important, articles referred to the MCCA program in the most laudatory terms, describing it variously as "a watershed" (1988), "a 'victory' for the elderly" (1987d), and protection "from the ravages of acute catastrophic illness" (1987a).

For all of its criticism of the financing, the *AARP Bulletin* coverage implied that the legislation was a good deal for all of the elderly (in terms of benefits received and costs), and consequently that there was no reason for any subgroup to oppose it. The effect of such reporting was probably similar to the effect the rest of the print and electronic media had: continuing attention on the part of the elderly to the legislation's financing, and misunderstanding of its implications for them personally.

In the floor debates shortly before the MCCA was passed in June 1988, a number of legislators worried openly that the elderly were unaware of its method of financing or failed to understand it. Senator Nickles wondered "how many American senior citizens are aware of the fact that this bill means they are going to have a surcharge placed on their tax" (U.S. Congress 1988, S7387). "There are many middle income senior citizens all over this Nation who are unaware that Congress plans to impose a 15 percent surcharge on them when they make out their income tax returns next April," asserted Representative Harris Fawell (U.S. Congress 1988, H3870). Even Senator Domenici, who voted in favor of the MCCA, feared that there would be a "backlash from older Americans when they find out exactly how costly these new benefits are" (U.S. Congress 1988, S7392).

Publicly, supporters strongly disagreed with such assessments, arguing that details of the legislation, including its financing, had received extensive attention during congressional hearings and floor debates. As Senator Bentsen would later say, "This [legislation] was not passed in the middle of the night, in the dark of night. It was not slipped through. This was done over two years" (U.S. Senate, Committee on Finance 1990, 93).

Moreover, according to MCCA advocates, the media and AARP had discussed the legislation frequently and in enough depth that the elderly were aware of its contents. Indeed, they interpreted the early public-opinion surveys as signaling widespread enthusiasm for the legislation among the elderly, and implicit acceptance of its method of financing. In Senator Bentsen's words, "The elderly are saying . . . we are willing to pay for these benefits to protect ourselves from the extraordinary, the catastrophic illness" (U.S. Congress 1988, S7414). Any remaining misunderstandings, the MCCA's architects believed, could be easily clarified through government and AARP public education campaigns.

Virtually none of the advocates envisioned that more than perfunctory efforts in this area would be necessary. With more than 60 percent of the elderly due to receive benefits from the MCCA program well in excess of personal costs, they reasoned, how could the vast majority of senior citizens not choose to support the program? From the view of advocates, the program's benefits were so apparent that the vast majority would immediately understand that supporting the program was in their best interest. The failure of many elderly citizens to agree with this assessment would emerge only later—as a total surprise to supporters.

5

SENIOR-CITIZEN OPINION AFTER PASSAGE OF THE MCCA

If viewed in the context of a simple political model where individuals are assumed to behave as self-interested actors, the Medicare Catastrophic Coverage Act of 1988 should have been popular legislation. Because almost two-thirds of the program's costs were concentrated on a minority of Medicare recipients liable for the supplemental premium, the vast majority of the elderly (more than 60 percent) were due to receive benefits in excess of their costs. Consequently, on this basis, a considerable majority could have been expected to support the program, and this support should have increased among the majority of "winners" as more became familiar with its provisions. Surprisingly, however, public-opinion data gathered after passage present a somewhat different picture.[1]

During the period following passage of the MCCA, opposition to the legislation among the elderly grew, and support dropped. This shift occurred even among those with the lowest incomes. The trend of increasing opposition and declining support is clearly evidenced by AARP surveys both before and after passage. By December 1988, support among the elderly had dropped from 91 percent to 65 percent, and opposition had increased to 21 percent (Table 5.1). Between December 1988 and February–March 1989, support dropped to 46 percent. Also notable was the steady increase in strong opposition, 4 percent in May 1988 increasing to 28 percent in August 1989.

1. The discussion in this section relies on microdata obtained from three surveys conducted on behalf of AARP following passage of the MCCA. All results cited are unweighted and pertain only to respondents age 65 and older. For discussion of these results, see also AARP Research and Data Resources Department 1989, and Straw 1990.

Table 5.1.   Support for and opposition to the MCCA among those 65 +

	Before Passage			After Passage		
	Apr. 1987	Sept. 1987	May 1988	Dec. 1988	Feb.–Mar. 1989	Aug. 1989
Strong support	—	57%	65%	32%	24%	16%
Some support	—	23%	26%	33%	22%	24%
Don't know/no opinion	5%	10%	4%	15%	24%	22%
Some opposition	—	3%	2%	10%	9%	9%
Strong opposition	—	8%	4%	11%	21%	28%
Total support	78%	80%	91%	65%	46%	40%
Total opposition	16%	11%	6%	21%	30%	37%
Difference[a]	+ 62	+ 69	+ 85	+ 44	+ 16	+ 3
N	128	136	172	657	1,011	395

SOURCE: Surveys commissioned by AARP. Numbers may not add to 100 due to rounding. All figures unweighted. See Straw 1990.

[a]Differences in opinion on last five surveys are significant at the $p < .01$ level.

This trend of increasing opposition and declining support for MCCA was present within high, moderate, and low income groups of elderly (Table 5.2).[2] Even among those with the lowest incomes, who stood to benefit most from the MCCA program in relation to their contributions, a 37-

2. For the analysis discussed herein, the elderly have been classified into three income groups based on likelihood of paying the supplemental premium and the degree to which MCCA benefits to individuals were likely to exceed personal costs. Because the supplemental premium took effect at different income levels, depending on whether a person was single or married (specifically, at approximately $15,000 and $25,000 respectively, see U.S. Senate, Committee on Finance 1990, 104–5), the income groups herein have been adjusted accordingly.

Thus, the low-income group includes single people with incomes below $10,000 and couples with a combined income of less than $20,000. This limit creates a group virtually all of whom would pay no supplemental premium and would receive program benefits well in excess of personal costs.

The moderate-income group contains single people with incomes from $10,000 to $20,000, and couples with incomes from $20,000 to $30,000. Here it is reasoned that the incomes of such people either made them liable for at least a small supplemental premium or provided them with a legitimate reason to believe that they might have to pay some premium. Although many in this group (including those who would pay some supplemental premium) stood to receive program benefits in excess of personal costs, the magnitude of such payoffs would be significantly less than those received by the low-income group.

Finally, the high-income elderly group includes singles with incomes above $20,000, and couples with incomes above $30,000. Virtually everyone in this group would pay significant amounts in supplemental premiums and receive program benefits that were exceeded by personal costs.

Table 5.2. Support for and opposition to the MCCA following passage, age 65 +, by income

	Dec. 1988	Feb.–Mar. 1989	Aug. 1989
Low income[a]			
Support	70%	52%	47%
Oppose	13%	23%	27%
Difference[b]	+57	+29	+20
N	255	402	165
Moderate income[a]			
Support	62%	49%	38%
Oppose	23%	33%	45%
Difference[c]	+29	+16	−7
N	151	241	99
High income[a]			
Support	63%	47%	38%
Oppose	31%	43%	57%
Difference[b]	+32	+5	−19
N	141	178	53

SOURCES: AARP Hamilton, Frederick & Schneiders Survey, December 1988; AARP EXCEL Poll 1, February–March 1989; AARP EXCEL Poll 2, August 1989. All figures unweighted.

[a]For an explanation of income cutoffs used to derive the income groups referred to here and in succeeding tables, see Chapter 5, footnote 2.
[b]Differences in opinion over time are significant at the p < .01 level.
[c]Differences in opinion over time are significant at the p < .05 level.

point shift from support to opposition occurred between December 1988 and August 1989. During this period, the proportion of those strongly opposed to the legislation also grew steadily in each income group (Table 5.3). This occurred even among the low-income elderly, where strong opposition increased fourfold over the eight-month period, from 5 percent to 21 percent.

Those rating themselves at least somewhat familiar with the MCCA opposed the legislation by wider margins than those who were unfamiliar. Further, during the survey period, differences in support widened between these two groups. This phenomenon occurred within all income groups, even among the elderly with the lowest incomes. While opposition to the MCCA increased both among those rating themselves familiar with the legislation and among those unfamiliar, during the survey period (see Table 5.4), it increased more precipitously in the former group (a 56-percentage-point swing toward opposition) than in the latter (a 31-percentage-point change). Indeed, opinions among those rating themselves familiar and

Table 5.3. Opposition to the MCCA following passage, age 65 +, overall and by income: Percentage strongly opposed

Expressing Strong Opposition	Dec. 1988	Feb.–Mar. 1989	Aug. 1989
All[a]	11%	21%	28%
Low income[a]	5%	15%	21%
Moderate income[a]	11%	20%	35%
High income[b]	22%	32%	42%

SOURCES: AARP Hamilton, Frederick & Schneiders Survey, December 1988; AARP EXCEL Poll 1, February–March 1989; AARP EXCEL Poll 2, August 1989. All figures unweighted.

[a]Differences over time are significant at the p < .01 level.
[b]Differences over time are significant at the p < .05 level.

Table 5.4. Support for and opposition to the MCCA among those rating themselves familiar (Fam.) and unfamiliar (Unf.) with the program, age 65 +

	Dec. 1988		Feb.–Mar. 1989		Aug. 1989	
	Fam.	Unf.	Fam.	Unf.	Fam.	Unf.
Strong support	32%	32%	28%	21%	17%	15%
Some support	35%	31%	21%	24%	22%	26%
Don't know/no answer	7%	24%	8%	38%	8%	37%
Some opposition	10%	9%	11%	8%	11%	8%
Strong opposition	16%	4%	32%	10%	43%	14%
Total support	67%	63%	49%	45%	39%	41%
Total opposition	26%	13%	43%	18%	54%	22%
Difference[a]	+41	+50	+6	+27	−15	+19
N	350	301	495	496	193	197

SOURCES: AARP Hamilton, Frederick & Schneiders Survey, December 1988; AARP EXCEL Poll 1, February–March 1989; AARP EXCEL Poll 2, August 1989. All figures unweighted.

[a]Differences in opinions of familiar and unfamiliar respondents within each survey are significant at the p < .01 level.

unfamiliar with the program diverged over time. In December 1988 the margin of support among elderly unfamiliar with the program was only 9 percentage points greater than that exhibited by familiar elderly (+50 to +41). By August 1989 this margin had grown to 34 percentage points (+19 to −15). Within income groups, these two trends were also present (see Table 5.5). Even among low-income elderly rating themselves familiar with the program, the margin of support dropped by 56 percentage points during the survey period (+68 in December 1988 to +12 in August 1989), a decline identical to that occurring among all familiar elderly. Also notable were the relative shifts in public opinion among familiar and unfamiliar

Table 5.5.   Support for and opposition to the MCCA among those rating
themselves familiar and unfamiliar with the program, age 65 +, by
income: Percentage supporting and opposing by level of familiarity

	Dec. 1988		Feb.–Mar. 1989		Aug. 1989	
	Fam.	Unf.	Fam.	Unf.	Fam.	Unf.
Low income						
Support	80%	63%	58%	48%	51%	43%
Oppose	12%	14%	34%	15%	39%	19%
Difference	+68	+49	+24	+33	+12	+24
N	105	146	163	231	67	97
Moderate income						
Support	62%	62%	46%	53%	35%	43%
Oppose	29%	12%	43%	21%	60%	26%
Difference	+33	+50	+3	+32	−25	+17
N	92	58	130	109	57	42
High income						
Support	62%	66%	48%	46%	35%	46%
Oppose	36%	18%	48%	30%	63%	38%
Difference	+26	+48	0	+16	−28	+8
N	101	39	134	44	40	13

SOURCES: AARP Hamilton, Frederick & Schneiders Survey, December 1988; AARP EXCEL
Poll 1, February–March 1989; AARP EXCEL Poll 2, August 1989. All figures unweighted.

elderly with low incomes. In December 1988 those rating themselves
familiar with the legislation were 19 percentage points more supportive
than their less-familiar counterparts. By August 1989 the former were 12
points *less* supportive than the latter.

*Knowledge of specific aspects of the costs and benefits of the MCCA
program was generally low among the elderly. The minority who had a
relatively high degree of knowledge were more likely to oppose the program
than those who did not. This relationship existed even among the elderly
with the lowest incomes.*[3]

AARP's February–March 1989 survey, which included fourteen true-

3. These results are supported by findings of a survey of 500 Medicare beneficiaries with
respect to the MCCA conducted in April–May 1989 by the Health Insurance Association of
America (HIAA). The survey, which included nine true-false questions comparable to those
contained in AARP's February–March 1989 poll, also found knowledge to be generally low
(with respondents answering an average of only 2.7 items correctly). In addition, analysis of
the HIAA microdata shows that those who had the most knowledge also exhibited the highest
degree of opposition to the MCCA. As in the AARP study, this was the case even among
respondents with the lowest incomes. For a general discussion of the HIAA survey, see Rice,
Desmond, and Gabel 1989.

false questions concerning specific aspects of the MCCA, found elderly respondents able to answer correctly an average of only four questions, and providing incorrect answers to an average of 3.5 items. Regarding specific aspects of the MCCA, on only two of the items (those pertaining to caps on physician charges and to the $4 monthly premium) were a majority of the elderly able to give a correct answer (see Table 5.6).

Among the minority of elderly demonstrating a relatively high degree of knowledge about the MCCA, opposition was higher by a margin of 14 percentage points than among those less knowledgeable (39 percent to 25

Table 5.6. Knowledge of specific aspects of the MCCA by income, age 65 +: Percentage answering each item correctly

Aspects	All	Low Income	Moderate Income	High Income
Covers all hospital expenses except deductible	21%	20%	21%	21%
One deductible maximum per year[a]	49%	42%	54%	57%
Caps physician charges	58%	59%	57%	57%
Doesn't cover physician charges beyond those approved[a]	19%	15%	21%	26%
Protects spouse from losing income and assets	35%	34%	32%	40%
Doesn't cover AIDS[a]	19%	15%	21%	26%
Doesn't cover long-term care[a]	32%	31%	27%	42%
Covers outpatient Rx[a]	22%	17%	27%	25%
Covers mammograms	34%	31%	35%	38%
Financed by elderly only[a]	18%	12%	18%	30%
$4 monthly premium paid by all	54%	51%	54%	60%
Supplemental premium paid by those owing $150 in federal taxes[a]	42%	31%	48%	60%
Upper limit exists on surtax[a]	32%	23%	37%	46%
Couple with $30,000 income would not pay maximum premium[a]	12%	6%	17%	20%
N	822	402	242	178

SOURCE: AARP EXCEL Poll 1, February–March 1989. All figures unweighted.

NOTE: See Appendix for exact wording of questions.

[a]Differences between income levels are significant at the p < .01 level.

percent opposed) (see Table 5.7). This relationship held even among the low-income elderly, where the margin of support among the knowledgeable group was 8 points lower than exhibited by those who were less knowledgeable.

In sum, then, during the period following passage, opposition to the MCCA increased significantly among the elderly and was more pronounced among those familiar with the program (in terms of self-assessed familiarity and demonstrated knowledge) than among those who were not. In the case of the senior citizens with moderate and high incomes, these results appear intuitively sensible. Because members of these two groups would probably pay more in premiums than they would receive in benefits from the program (or had some reason to believe this might occur), opposition to the program could be expected to increase over time and in response to increasing familiarity in these groups. This is what appears to have occurred.

In the case of the elderly with low incomes, the survey results are difficult to explain. If this group had behaved in accord with their economic self-interest, support for the MCCA should have increased over time as they became familiar with the program, and should have increased more precipitously among those rating themselves familiar with the program or demonstrating knowledge of it. Instead, just the opposite was true. During the survey period, opposition increased generally among the low-income elderly, the most pronounced increases occurring among those who were most familiar with the program. How can this be explained? The answer appears to lie in a number of misperceptions held by the low-income elderly with respect to the costs and benefits of the legislation. Specifically:

Perceptions of how the MCCA's benefits and costs would affect one personally appeared to be highly influential for the elderly in deciding whether to support or oppose the program. In general, perceptions of the low-income elderly with respect to such issues varied relatively little from those in the higher-income groups. The AARP surveys found consistent and considerable hostility toward the legislation's costs. The December 1988 survey, for example, found 61 percent agreement with the statement "The cost of the program to older Americans is too high considering the benefits they receive." Although opposition to the MCCA was relatively low in the December survey (21 percent), it was closely related to respondents' assessments of the costs and benefits of the program. While 57 percent in the December survey agreed that the costs they would pay under the program were worth it to them personally, "considering the benefits," an AARP analysis notes that "those supporting the legislation were three times

Table 5.7. Support for and opposition to the MCCA by level of demonstrated knowledge and by income, age 65 +, February–March 1989

Knowledge Level:[c]	All[a]		Low Income		Moderate Income[b]		High Income	
	High	Low	High	Low	High	Low	High	Low
Strong support	21%	29%	19%	31%	22%	26%	23%	25%
Some support	27%	22%	31%	21%	26%	24%	24%	24%
Don't know/no opinion	13%	24%	23%	27%	9%	24%	5%	15%
Some opposition	10%	10%	6%	8%	11%	13%	12%	10%
Strong opposition	29%	15%	21%	13%	32%	13%	37%	27%
Total support	48%	51%	50%	52%	48%	50%	47%	49%
Total opposition	39%	25%	27%	21%	43%	26%	49%	37%
Difference	+9	+26	+23	+31	+5	+24	−2	+12
N	305	516	119	283	97	144	89	89

SOURCE: AARP EXCEL Poll 1, February–March 1989. All figures unweighted.

[a]Differences between high and low knowledge are significant at the p < .01 level.
[b]Differences between high and low knowledge are significant at the p < .05 level.
[c]Knowledge levels were determined by the difference between correct and incorrect answers given to fourteen true-false items pertaining to the MCCA (see Table 5.6 for a description of specific items). Those answering two or more correct than incorrect are judged highly knowledgeable, those scoring below this level are said to have low knowledge of program.

as likely to believe the benefits were worth the costs to them (72 percent versus 23 percent)" (Straw 1990, 9).

In the same survey, income level per se appears to have had minimal effects on satisfaction with the costs and benefits. For example, while 51 percent of high-income elderly agreed that the program's costs were worth it to them personally, considering the benefits, the percentage of low-income elderly agreeing with the statement (58 percent) was only marginally higher.[4] Similarly, the percentage of high-income and low-income elderly agreeing that the program's costs to older Americans were too high considering the benefits (60 and 64 percent respectively) were roughly even.[5]

Elderly dissatisfaction with the supplemental premium appeared to underlie many perceptions of the program's costs and was crucial in driving opposition. Further, this dissatisfaction extended even to the elderly with the lowest incomes, virtually all of whom were unlikely to pay any surtax. For example, AARP's December 1988 survey found half of all senior citizens rating positively the statement "Everyone eligible for Medicare who pays more than $150 in federal taxes will pay (a separate, supplemental) an extra premium based on the amount of tax they owe." Among the low-income elderly, a virtually identical 51 percent rated the provision positively.[6]

Nine months later, in AARP's August 1989 survey, displeasure with the supplemental premium had only grown. Asked to cite major reasons for opposition to the program, 86 percent of all elderly opponents, including 84 percent of all low-income opponents, agreed that "the supplemental premium of $22.50 for each $150 of income tax owed is too high."[7] Another example of the widespread animosity of the elderly toward the supplemental premium was seen in that same survey when all respondents (not just opponents) were presented with seven proposed reforms and asked whether they would make them more or less likely to support the program. The proposal to pair a decrease in the supplemental premium with an increase in the monthly premium was by far the most popular of the reforms (see Table 5.8), with a margin of 5 to 1 stating that such a change would make them more likely to support than to oppose. Even those with the lowest incomes supported this change by only a slightly smaller margin,

---

4. Differences in responses of the three income groups are insignificant (p > .10).
5. Differences in responses of the three income groups are insignificant (p > .10).
6. Differences in responses of the three income groups are insignificant (p > .10).
7. Differences in responses of the three income groups are insignificant (p > .10).

Table 5.8. Impact of proposed changes of the MCCA on support or opposition among those 65 +, overall and by income: Percentage supporting or opposing proposed changes

Proposed Change	All		Low Income		Moderate Income		High Income	
	Supp.	Opp.	Supp.	Opp.	Supp.	Opp.	Supp.	Opp.
Increase monthly premium to reduce supplemental premium	37%	28%	34%	28%	38%	32%	42%	22%
Decrease in supplemental premium paired with increase in basic premium[a]	53%	12%	47%	11%	54%	18%	71%	6%
Shift costs of hospital insurance benefits to payroll taxes	37%	24%	33%	23%	37%	27%	46%	21%
Make catastrophic and Medicare B a package that is voluntary[a]	31%	21%	30%	17%	30%	23%	36%	28%
Increase deductible for prescriptions to avoid adding to program costs	30%	30%	28%	32%	33%	29%	33%	25%
Raise cap on out-of-pocket expenses to reduce supplemental premium	25%	39%	28%	37%	19%	43%	26%	40%
Add limited LTC home-care benefit; finance through increased payroll taxes of those with $45,000 + incomes	44%	26%	46%	21%	43%	29%	40%	32%
N	307		158		99		50	

SOURCE: AARP EXCEL Poll 2, August 1989. All figures unweighted.

[a]Differences between income levels are significant at the p < .05 level.

more than 4 to 1, even though the reformed program was almost certain to cost them more.

Throughout the period following passage, the elderly who believed that the program duplicated benefits they already had were more likely to oppose the MCCA than those who did not. AARP's December 1988 and February–March 1989 surveys provide evidence on this issue. Opposition to the MCCA was approximately 30 percent higher in both surveys among those who believed that the MCCA's benefits duplicated coverage they already had (see Table 5.9). It is not surprising that the proportions of those believing they had duplicative coverage rose with income.[8]

So far, the factors hypothesized as influencing public opinion on the MCCA—income, self-rated familiarity, demonstrated knowledge, attitudes concerning program costs and benefits, the supplemental premium, and possession of duplicative coverage—have been examined separately. In an attempt to test their relative influence on senior-citizen opinions of the MCCA program, three multivariate analyses were undertaken using the

Table 5.9. Support for and opposition to the MCCA among those 65 + who believed the program duplicated coverage they currently had, compared with those who did not

	Dec. 1988		Feb.–Mar. 1989	
	Had Coverage	No Coverage	Had Coverage	No Coverage
Strong support	28%	34%	19%	25%
Some support	29%	34%	22%	22%
Don't know/No opinion	11%	17%	12%	28%
Some opposition	13%	8%	15%	8%
Strong opposition	20%	6%	32%	17%
Total support	57%	68%	41%	47%
Total opposition	33%	14%	47%	25%
Difference[a]	+24	+54	−6	+22
N	209	418	233	778

SOURCE: AARP Hamilton, Frederick & Schneiders Survey, December 1988; AARP EXCEL Poll 1, February–March 1989. All figures unweighted.

[a]Differences in opinion between those possessing and not possessing coverage within each survey are statistically significant at the p < .01 level.

8. In both surveys, 47 percent of the high-income elderly believed they had such coverage, while less than 25 percent of the low-income elderly responded affirmatively. Differences between responses of the three income groups are statistically significant (p < .01).

December 1988 and February–March 1989 surveys. In the analyses (detailed in the Appendix), perceptions concerning the effects of program benefits and costs on one personally, opinions regarding the supplemental premium, and beliefs about whether one already had such coverage are found to be highly influential in explaining opposition to the MCCA. By contrast, income, self-rated familiarity, and levels of demonstrated knowledge about the program have little or no independent effect on opinions.[9]

Thus, the multivariate analyses yield two main findings. First, perceived self-interest of the elderly was highly influential in decisions to oppose the MCCA. Assessments related to different aspects of the benefits and costs were pivotal in influencing opinions. Second, Americans age 65 and older in general, and those with low incomes in particular, continually misunderstood a number of the program's key aspects, especially those concerning the supplemental premium.

These findings, combined with the trend of increasing opposition by senior citizens of all income levels, detailed earlier, raise vexing questions: How did the elderly come to believe that supporting the program was not in their best interest? And why were advocates of the legislation unable to change those perceptions? Explaining this puzzle is the subject of Chapter 6.

9. These results conflict with those of Day (1993), who found self-interest not to be significantly related to attitudes toward the MCCA (although increasing income was found to be a significant predictor of negative opinions about the program). Such discrepancies might be attributable to differences in the comprehensiveness of survey data analyzed. Specifically, Day's data, which come from a November 1989 ABC News/*Washington Post* survey not focused primarily on the MCCA, contain only a few items relating to the program, and only two concerning perceptions of direct self-interest (believing one had to pay more for benefits, or believing one had supplemental health coverage). Absent are a number of variables addressing this issue that are present in the survey data I analyze, including attitudes toward specific aspects of the program, particularly the supplemental premium; knowledge and perceptions of these features; and assessments of how much one would owe under the new program, how many people would benefit, and whether one would actually receive benefits.

6

REPEAL OF THE MCCA

By November 1988, a mere five months after passage of the MCCA, senior citizens were in open revolt against the program, particularly its supplemental premium. Although much of the early opposition to the program appeared to emerge without prompting,[1] a number of interest groups—the most famous being the National Committee to Preserve Social Security and Medicare—quickly organized to exploit such sentiment. Over the next twelve months senior citizens besieged Congress with thousands of pieces of mail and angrily confronted lawmakers on their trips home to demand repeal.

The virulence of this reaction surprised even congressional veterans who had supported the legislation. "This is the most intense I've ever seen senior citizens in my 10 years in Congress," said Representative Robert Matsui in December 1988, "and it's still heating up" (Birnbaum and Davidson 1988). Senator John Warner remarked, "In my 11 years in the U.S. Senate I have never dealt with an issue which has met with such unrelenting opposition" (U.S. Congress 1989, S6322). "I have never seen anything like the outcry, yes, across this country from the elderly," said Representative Barbara Kennelly (U.S. Congress 1989, H6570). Describing the visit of one con-

---

1. The media were virtually silent on the MCCA during the second half of 1988. Following the Rose Garden signing ceremony for the legislation on July 1, the three networks failed to air even one story on the new legislation over this time span. In the print media, coverage of senior-citizen reaction was only marginally more expansive after July 2, with the *New York Times* (Tolchin 1988) and the *Wall Street Journal* (Birnbaum and Davidson 1988) running only one news story each, while the *Washington Post* (1988c) printed a single editorial on the topic.

gressman to his district, *New York Times* reporter Robin Toner (1989) wrote that constituents appeared to be obsessed with the MCCA. "Other issues that have consumed Congress for months, issues that were widely expected to arouse people, barely registered," she wrote.

The culmination of the outrage over the program occurred on August 19, 1989, when a group of several dozen senior citizens accosted Representative Dan Rostenkowski, chairman of the House Committee on Ways and Means and an influential supporter of the legislation, following a meeting with community leaders in his district who opposed the legislation. Shouting "Coward!" "Recall!" and "Impeach!" the crowd surrounded Rostenkowski's car, beating it with picket signs and pounding on its windows. A few moments later a shaken Rostenkowski was forced to flee the scene on foot. Replayed a number of times on the network news, the incident came to be viewed as the most vivid illustration of how displeased the elderly were with the legislation (*Newsweek* 1989, 42–43; Rovner 1989i, 2316).

As senior-citizen opposition escalated, the program's architects in Congress struggled to fashion a coherent and understandable defense. From their perspective, complaints arose from two sources: a vocal minority of affluent elderly who balked at assuming their fair, if disproportionate, share of the costs, and a confused majority who mistakenly believed that they too would be subject to the supplemental premium, possibly even the 1989 maximum of $800. MCCA architects placed much of the blame for the latter group's confusion on the efforts of the National Committee, which, they charged, had spread misleading information about the program in numerous direct-mail solicitations.

Program supporters initially believed that the anger of senior citizens could be quelled through intensive public-education efforts. "When you go out and explain to people what's in the bill, they're much happier about it, even if they don't like the financing," said one AARP lobbyist (Rovner 1988h, 3451). "Our experience is that those who figure [MCCA's financing] out are inevitably surprised at how little [the cost] is," asserted AARP legislative director John Rother (Kosterlitz 1988). In an attempt to explain the law, the federal government in October 1988 mailed sixteen-page handbooks on the MCCA to each of Medicare's 32 million beneficiaries (*Washington Post* 1989b). Even more intense were AARP's efforts, which included a special newsletter, a video, and trained volunteers who were "to go out to the hinterlands and tame the consternation," in the words of one organization official (Birnbaum and Davidson 1988). Congressional supporters sought to reinforce these efforts by emphasizing that the program would provide the vast majority of elderly beneficiaries with significant benefits at minimal personal cost.

Unfortunately for advocates, none of these actions proved successful in rallying elderly support for the legislation. (In fact, such efforts arguably exacerbated opposition.) As criticism of the program continued to escalate during 1989, congressional supporters tried a number of times to decrease supplemental premiums in an attempt to save various portions of the program's benefits. These efforts, which continued through the summer and the fall, continually met with failure as the act's costs soared beyond projections; as Congress refused to broaden the program's financing; as advocates for the elderly fought attempts to decrease the progressivity of its premiums; and as the elderly refused to pay for even a significantly scaled-down package of benefits. Unable to fix the legislation, Congress in October and November 1989 voted by wide majorities to repeal outright virtually the entire package passed eighteen months earlier.[2]

The underlying causes of the increasing opposition to the MCCA on the part of the elderly after the legislation was passed, and the continued inability of advocates to change such attitudes, are numerous and complex. One explanation, advanced mainly by opponents in Congress, has to do with the program's failure to provide comprehensive coverage for the most severe financial catastrophe feared by senior citizens—the cost of long-term care. According to Representative Harris Fawell, the MCCA failed to recognize this "highest priority." Long-term care, he said "is a benefit all Americans, young and old alike want, and the law does not even address it in the most minimal of ways" (U.S. Congress 1989, H6570). Said Representative Dan Burton: "The No. 1 health care concern for the elderly is long-term nursing care and long-term in home care and the Catastrophic Care Act didn't offer any solutions to these serious problems" (U.S. Congress 1989, H6575). Said Senator James McClure, "This law was misnamed from the beginning. It should not be called the Medicare Catastrophic Care Act. . . . The catastrophe that most senior citizens fear the most is not prescription drug costs. It is not extended hospitalization. It is nursing home care" (U.S. Congress 1989, S12871).[3]

2. A few minor provisions of the MCCA were not repealed, the most notable being spousal-impoverishment protection for long-term nursing-home patients. For a discussion of other remaining benefits, see U.S. House, Committee on Ways and Means 1990, 201–2; Rovner 1989m, 3239.

3. Because these criticisms arose mainly from conservative Republicans opposed to a major federal role in long-term care, they infuriated MCCA supporters, many of whom had devoted years of effort to this cause. In June 1989 Senate Majority Leader George Mitchell,

Such arguments contain more than an element of truth. The MCCA did not provide for comprehensive coverage of long-term care, and the use of the term "catastrophic" in the legislation's title could have misled many elderly into believing it did. However, two factors mitigate against this hypothesis as the main explanation for the increased elderly opposition.

First, the survey data set forth in the preceding chapter indicate that although the absence of a comprehensive long-term-care benefit probably helped fuel opposition, unhappiness with the program's supplemental premiums (albeit in many cases misguided) always exerted a significantly stronger influence (see Table 5.8 and the multivariate analyses detailed in the Appendix). Second, while the MCCA did not provide comprehensive coverage for long-term custodial care, it did offer a number of benefits that constituted significant progress toward that goal. Provisions concerning skilled nursing facilities, home health care, and respite care had been critical in the AARP's initial decision to support the program (see Chapter 3). AARP's leaders and many MCCA supporters in Congress viewed these benefits as the foundation for future legislation.[4] From the perspective of these advocates, the increasing opposition was a consequence not so much of its failure to provide comprehensive coverage for long-term care but rather of their failure to persuade senior citizens of the presence and the significance of these more limited benefits.

In contrast to the opponents, program supporters generally attributed the growing displeasure of senior citizens to the activities of one group—the National Committee to Preserve Social Security and Medicare. According to conventional wisdom, this organization constituted "the main engine behind the mailstorm" that descended on Congress (Weisberg 1989, 11), "incited the elderly" (Tolchin 1989f), "deserved a good deal of blame" for the failure to understand the program (Rich 1989d), and "played an enormous role in bringing down the legislation" (personal interview with congressional staffer). "I find a high degree of confusion among seniors concerning the program," elaborated Representative Pete Stark, the most forceful proponent of this position (Tolchin 1989f). "That confusion was

one of the legislation's major architects, bitterly noted: "As carefully as we have researched the record, with a single exception . . . not one of the other senators who have during this debate expressed such concern for the elderly participated in any way in the effort to deal with that problem" (Senator Paul Simon, he noted, was the exception) (Rovner 1989e, 1401).

4. It is ironic that, following the MCCA's passage, the increasing costs of the SNF benefit led many to question whether the program would remain truly self-financing. For further discussion, see the section later in this chapter concerning congressional efforts to save the program.

exacerbated by a fraudulent campaign by the owners of the mail order firm," continued Stark, "this . . . operation, whose sole interest is to generate mailing lists and membership fees. They plied their trade on the most fragile members of our society, who are easily confused, frightened and misled."

Such allegations were correct in two important respects. First, following passage of the MCCA, the National Committee's appeals to seniors continually distorted important details concerning the legislation's financing. (This, of course, was merely a continuation of the group's activities before the legislation became law. For details, see Chapter 4.) During the second half of 1988 and 1989, the organization sent its 4.5 million members numerous letters attacking the program in shrill, virtually hysterical terms. "A special tax on senior citizens! Have you ever heard of anything so outrageous in your life?" exclaimed one appeal (Hosenball 1989). Another began: "1989 INCOME TAXES FOR MILLIONS OF SENIORS WILL INCREASE BY UP TO $1,600.000 ($800.00 FOR SINGLES)—IT'S A TAX ON SENIORS ONLY AND IT MUST BE STOPPED!" (Weisberg 1989, 11). Although many of these appeals included accurate information about the MCCA, including the fact that the surtax was limited to relatively wealthy seniors, this information appeared "lower down in the text below the eye catching headlines" (Hosenball 1989).[5]

Second, the National Committee's appeals prompted significant numbers of senior citizens (their income levels unknown) to contact representatives in opposition to the MCCA, and these efforts in turn influenced Congress's decision to repeal the legislation. In the months preceding the repeal, Congress was deluged with literally thousands of pieces of mail protesting the program. Although much of it appeared to consist of postcards bearing preprinted messages from the National Committee, the sheer volume probably caused many in Congress to reconsider their support (Hosenball 1989). Among the congressional staffers I interviewed, none sought to downplay the National Committee's role in the repeal. Indeed, the group loomed so large in their assessments that it was the only source of organized opposition any volunteered.

But, the National Committee to Preserve Social Security and Medicare was by no means alone in opposing the MCCA. Following passage, a wide

5. The National Committee's incendiary appeals to senior citizens appear to have been confined to its direct-mail literature. Although hostile toward the MCCA, this organization's press releases (National Committee 1989c and 1989e), letters to elected officials (National Committee 1989b and 1989f), and newsletter, *Saving Social Security* (National Committee 1989a and 1989d), adopted a distinctly more balanced, less strident tone.

array of organizations emerged to demand repeal. A few of these groups were little more than direct-mail shops intent on imitating the National Committee's tactics in pursuit of financial gain.[6] Most, though, were far more reputable with respect to motives and methods. They included well-established organizations representing retired public employees and military personnel. Members of these groups accounted for a vast majority of the 7 million elderly citizens (23 percent of all Medicare recipients) who already received partially or fully subsidized coverage from current or past employers for at least a portion of the benefits offered by the MCCA (Rovner 1989l, 2715).[7] Two of the earliest opponents of the legislation—the National Association of Retired Federal Employees (500,000 members) and the Retired Officers Association (350,000 members)—labored through 1989 to mobilize other organizations with significant numbers of senior citizens in similar circumstances to join the campaign for repeal. By August 1989 their Coalition for Affordable Health Care included forty-four groups representing a combined membership of 19 million persons—many though by no means all of them elderly. While a number of retiree and senior-citizen groups were part of the coalition, membership also included a number of powerful public-employee unions, such as the National Association of Letter Carriers and the National Association of Government Employees (see U.S. Congress 1989, S6314, for a complete list).

Following passage, grass-roots organizations founded specifically to fight the legislation also emerged. Many of these entities—bearing such names as Seniors Against the Surtax, the Coalition for Repeal of the Medicare Catastrophic Care Act, and the Committee for Repeal of the Catastrophic Health Act of 1988—appear to have been largely storefront operations consisting of little more than a few dozen members and a letterhead. The

6. These included the Conservative Caucus under the direction of political activist Howard Phillips, and the Seniors Coalition Against the Tax, a creation of conservative direct-mail wizard Richard Viguerie. During 1989 the former sent letters proclaiming the MCCA "unconstitutional" (Weisberg 1989) and warning seniors that their taxes may have "increased by as much as $800 per year" (Hosenball 1989). Donations permitted the organization "to hire full-time lobbyists and coordinators to support repeal of the Catastrophic Coverage Act." During the same period, the Viguerie group mailed senior citizens mock 1989 tax returns that warned of "a catastrophic tax of up to $800 or $1,600 per couple this year alone" (ibid.). Contributions allowed the group to send out a "blizzard of petitions" opposing the act.

7. Although not widely known or understood by Medicare enrollees at the time, "only one-third of MCCA's benefits would have overlapped with benefits already covered by Medigap" (Moon 1993, 132). Unfortunately, "those who would be asked to pay the most under the government plan were those who had the best coverage at the lowest cost through their own private arrangements" (Moon 1993, 133).

major exception was the Seniors Coalition Against the Catastrophic Act (SCACA), a Las Vegas–based group founded in August 1988 by Daniel Hawley, a sixty-four-year-old airline pilot. A self-described "national clearing house" for seniors "unrepresented by national organizations" or belonging to "large national organizations which are not listening to the demands of their membership" (U.S. Senate, Committee on Finance 1990, 123), the SCACA led a petition drive on behalf of repeal in 1988 and 1989, which garnered significant media coverage as well as 326,427 signatures (Birnbaum and Davidson 1988; Diegmueller 1989; Rovner 1989c, 1329). The organization was also credited with prompting the Nevada congressional delegation (both senators and representatives) to become early and outspoken opponents of the program (Rovner 1988h, 3452).

In short, organized opposition to the MCCA extended well beyond the efforts of the National Committee to Preserve Social Security and Medicare.[8] The presence of numerous groups fighting for repeal appears to indicate that the antipathy of seniors to the legislation would have remained significant even in the absence of this organization. In fact, the MCCA gave elderly citizens who had relatively high incomes (who were probably disproportionately represented in these groups) ample reason for being unhappy. The surtaxes the MCCA imposed on such persons, combined with the fact that many already had such coverage at little or no cost, ensured that organized opposition to the program would have remained intense under any circumstances.

While the direct-mail campaign of the National Committee and other organizations added to the confusion of some elderly people with lower incomes, understanding of the program and support for it among that group may not have been appreciably higher had there been no such efforts. This is because before the MCCA was passed the program had been sold as offering significant benefits to *all* senior citizens regardless of income. To the extent that a significant segment of the elderly perceived the program as a "bad deal" for themselves personally and organized to fight for repeal, it is likely that those with lower incomes too would harbor similar doubts and suspicions. These attitudes would probably hold regardless of attempts by program advocates to persuade them otherwise. This is what apparently occurred in the case of the MCCA.

8. According to one analysis (Houston 1989), "Congress did not take seriously a flood of mail opposing the bill because the outpouring was prompted by . . . the National Committee. . . . Legislators began to listen only when they got earfuls of protest from their constituents when they visited their districts in August [1989]."

Ultimately, the failure of advocates to address clearly and honestly the redistributive implications of the legislation's financing (more than the exploits of the National Committee) may account for increasing opposition of senior citizens and the misperceptions of the program held by lower-income seniors.[9]

Previous chapters have revealed that while the legislation's architects embraced the concept of progressive financing as a means of reducing the generous Medicare subsidies garnered by the wealthy elderly, they sought publicly to downplay the presence of redistribution in the MCCA. In doing so, advocates chose to proceed in the tradition of previous social-insurance policy-making where efforts to obscure the transfer of dollars from wealthy to poor participants had effectively preserved public support for programs that had significant welfare components. Consequently, before the MCCA was passed, its supporters generally emphasized the program's benefits and downplayed its costs. More significantly, is that they made little attempt to discourage the perception (widely implied in the media) that on balance all beneficiaries stood to benefit considerably from the legislation.

The problem was that the latter claim was not true. Unlike Social Security and Medicare, where payroll taxes of workers and the presence of general revenues made participation beneficial (in a benefit-cost sense) for even the wealthiest beneficiaries, the MCCA program was in reality a zero-sum game where a significant portion of benefits of low-income and middle-income beneficiaries would be paid for by a minority of those with high incomes. As a result, for the first time in the history of American social insurance the most affluent participants would, on average, get back less than they contributed (in terms of the MCCA alone). Further, the highly progressive financing mechanism of the MCCA—40 percent of the beneficiaries would pay 82 percent of the legislation's cost (U.S. Congress 1989, S12840)—made the redistributive intent underlying the program too obvious to be overlooked. Unfortunately, for MCCA architects, this would be apparent only in retrospect. Before passage, it was believed that the program could be justified to the elderly and to the general public in terms similar to Social Security and Medicare, as a program beneficial to all participants.

Only after criticism of the MCCA began to mount did program advocates

9. An internal AARP memo (1989b) employed similar language ("Financing rationale was not explained honestly or clearly") to explain the repeal. However, this factor was only one of "Twelve Deadly Sins of Catastrophic" cited in the memo. By contrast, my study places significantly heavier emphasis on this explanation as a cause of the program's downfall.

make a concerted effort to explain the redistributive implications of the program's financing. Indeed, clearly frustrated at their inability to persuade the vast majority of elderly that the program offered them significant benefits at minimal cost, the legislation's architects and supporters now sought to depict redistribution as the program's raison d'être.[10] In the process, program advocates abandoned their insistence that all senior citizens would benefit financially from the program—a line of argument that was becoming increasingly implausible. Instead, they began to assert, in the words of House Ways and Means Chairman Dan Rostenkowski, that the bill "was primarily designed to help those elderly who did not have additional insurance and whose income was just high enough to keep them from Medicaid eligibility" (U.S. Congress 1989, H6583).

According to the MCCA architects, the most strident demands for repeal of the program came from a small group of affluent seniors who were motivated by greed and selfishness. "What you have is the wealthier people not wanting to pay an additional premium and wanting it to be more heavily subsidized by the other taxpayers in this country," explained Senator Lloyd Bentsen (Rasky 1989). "You have a very vocal minority sounding off." Representative Pete Stark argued that supporters of the legislation were "being stampeded by . . . a small group of wealthy seniors, to deny needed benefits to a majority of seniors" (Rovner 1989k, 2637). More caustic were the remarks of Senator Robert Packwood, who said that

10. Notably absent from this effort was AARP. According to one high official I interviewed, the organization privately supported the MCCA's progressive method of financing for pragmatic reasons ("Otherwise the poor couldn't afford the benefits"), but was unwilling to portray itself as "being married to" any mechanism that imposed all program costs on the elderly. Failure to uphold the latter principle publicly would undermine what the AARP termed "the 'spread the risk' social-insurance principles upon which Medicare was founded" (AARP 1989a). From the perspective of the organization's leaders, their acceptance of the MCCA's elderly-only financing mechanism was a one-time concession reluctantly made in exchange for the legislation's benefits. "The financing mechanism was not our proposal," said John Rother, AARP's legislative director, in comments echoed by AARP and its representatives on numerous occasions following the MCCA's passage. "There were compromises and negotiations. You do the best you can. We supported it at the end" (Tolchin 1988). So as criticism of the program's supplemental premium mounted during 1988 and 1989, AARP would say only that the "financing should be broadened . . . through the inclusion of all state and local government workers in Medicare and an increase in the tobacco tax" (AARP 1989a). But because the AARP stood virtually alone among senior-citizen interest groups in defending the legislation's benefits as worthwhile and necessary when the program came under attack, the MCCA's congressional architects appeared to harbor little ill-will toward the organization for publicly attempting to distance itself from the program's financing mechanism. Indeed, legislators and congressional staffers interviewed dismissed AARP's public statements on the MCCA as little more than minimal efforts to pacify disgruntled members.

those protesting the legislation "all live in Sun City [Arizona] and . . . have incomes of $30,000 or $35,000 or $40,000 a year" (U.S. Congress 1989, S6174). "I do not think," he continued, "that it is unfair or unethical or wrong to ask those of us who are a little bit more privileged to give a little extra to take care of those who are a little less privileged. I hope we do not bend to those who are better off." Even Senator Alan Simpson, a conservative Republican who had played little role in the passage beyond voting to support the legislation, expressed his dismay "that the whole United States has been swung on its tail by five percent of their most fortunate cogenarians who don't want to pay for these benefits" (U.S. Congress 1989, S12861).

To justify the steep supplemental premiums the MCCA imposed on the high-income elderly, program advocates sought to publicize the generous government subsidies Medicare recipients were already receiving.[11] "The fact is that Medicare will continue to be an insurance bargain for its enrollees even *including* those who will pay the maximum supplemental premium," argued Representative Gradison (1989). "That person who pays the full amount is still getting a bargain," observed Senate Minority Leader Bob Dole (U.S. Congress 1989, S6297). "The least subsidized high-income enrollee," he noted, "will still realize a subsidy [in 1989] of $800 a year so he or she is still paying for [only] 79 percent of the benefits that he or she uses." Even for those paying the maximum premium, "there will still be a subsidy out of general revenue," noted Senator Bentsen (U.S. Congress 1989, S6296). "Try to find me a comparable buy for that one, with the intensity of coverage, the depth of coverage, the expanse of coverage, and buy it on the market for that," he added.

11. Their chief weapons in this battle were statistics from the Congressional Budget Office (1988b; 1988c; 1989) detailing the level of Medicare subsidies garnered by the elderly in the absence and the presence of the MCCA. The CBO's analyses acknowledged that "the incremental effect" of the MCCA for the most affluent 30 to 40 percent of the elderly "subject to the supplemental premium" was "negative" (1989, ix). In other words, these enrollees would "face new premium costs in excess of their new expected benefits under the act" (1988c, 3). At the same time, though, the CBO (1989, ix) emphasized that even with the MCCA all seniors could still "expect to receive more benefits in total under Medicare than the value of their contributions," that "even for those enrollees paying the maximum supplemental premiums each year, the [annual lifetime] subsidy will be more than $1,300 a year." These subsidies existed for two reasons. First, payroll contributions of the wealthiest beneficiaries covered only 61 percent of benefits received through Medicare A (1989, 30). Second, premiums for basic Part B benefits were set at only 25 percent of program costs. Throughout 1989, congressional supporters regularly cited these facts and others contained in the CBO analyses to argue that the surtaxes were fair and consequently that the affluent elderly had no legitimate grievance against the program's method of financing.

To underline this point, Bentsen and Gradison each proposed that Medicare beneficiaries be permitted to opt out of the program if they also agreed to drop Part B coverage under Medicare. With 75 percent of Part B costs paid by the government, beneficiaries would discover that Medicare was, in Bentsen's words, "really a bargain" (Rich 1989c), "the best buy in town" (Rich 1989a). "Anybody who can count to 10 and put their shoes and socks on won't opt out," agreed Representative Stark (Rovner 1989g, 1860).

Although Bentsen's and Gradison's proposals were ultimately rejected by Congress (see the concluding section of this chapter), efforts by MCCA architects to invoke the redistributive rationale underlying the program were enthusiastically endorsed in the editorial pages and op-ed columns of major publications. Echoing the arguments of congressional supporters, many commentaries emphasized the significant government subsidies that affluent senior citizens would continue to garner even under the MCCA. More notable, though, were the biting criticisms they leveled at high-income seniors. "There's little reason to sympathize with the aggrieved affluent elderly," wrote the *New York Times* (1989) in an editorial that termed their complaints "short-sighted and narrow-minded." The *Washington Post* (1989) declared, "It is craven of Congress to yield so quickly to a basically comfortable group for whom Medicare remains a good deal—they get back more than they put in—and good of the committees and the administration to try to preserve as much as they can of the benefits and progressivity." Writing in the *New Republic*, Phillip Longman (1989, 18) asked, "So long as we continue to provide enormous subsidies to the affluent elderly, why shouldn't they help pay for the poor of their generation?" He concluded: "The affluent elderly must realize that they may pay a price for their selfishness."

This perspective was also present in network television's coverage of the MCCA. A September 18, 1989, story by ABC's Sheila Kast attributed the impending demise of the MCCA to the greed of affluent seniors. In her assessment, it was "the more well-to-do elderly who are sending their representatives in Washington a powerful political message—Don't make us pay even if it means depriving everyone of catastrophic care." Following the story, ABC anchorman Peter Jennings echoed the substance of Kast's remarks:

Congress, having first decided that those who can afford it should pick up some of the burden of catastrophic insurance, is now going to be pressured into changing its mind because those who are deemed able to pay or have other insurance are violently opposed—which may well mean that because five million elderly people are angry as many as 18 million may suffer.

Another example of such reporting appeared following the October 7, 1989, Senate vote to repeal the MCCA's supplemental premium. Speaking from Capitol Hill, NBC reporter Andrea Mitchell summarized the day's events by remarking, "Some say a vocal minority of seniors, coupled with congressional cowardice, have ruined it for the truly needy."

Possibly even more vivid than the comments of these journalists were the images selected to reinforce them. In such stories, affluent elderly were pictured in two contexts: enjoying their retirement years at the golf course and angrily accosting their elected representatives (for example, the Rostenkowski incident). By contrast, potential MCCA beneficiaries were depicted through a procession of what Binstock (1983) has called "compassionate stereotypes" intended to elicit sympathy from the general public. They included a woman with a brain tumor (according to NBC's Bob Kerr, January 10, 1989, the MCCA would cover all her hospital expenses), a stroke victim (if the MCCA were repealed, said ABC's George Strait on September 18, 1989, "she could lose her independence and end up on welfare"), and an elderly couple burdened by high medical expenses ("Ms. Smith doesn't take her medicine each day because she can't afford to," explained CBS's Bob Schieffer on October 2, 1989, alluding to the importance of the prescription-drug benefit). The subtext of these images was unmistakable—the greed of a few affluent senior citizens was to blame for the downfall of a program that offered a large majority medical benefits they desperately needed.

Unfortunately for MCCA advocates, their belated efforts to address the redistributive implications of the program's financing probably served only to increase rather than dampen the opposition to the program. From the perspective of the affluent elderly, the explanations of supporters likely constituted an exercise in deception. What had been touted as an unmitigated benefit for all senior citizens, they learned, was in fact a bad deal for those with relatively high incomes. Further, as discussed above, for many it was a doubly bad deal because they already had such coverage at little or no cost from employers.[12] Attempts to place the effects of the MCCA in the

12. Kosterlitz (1989b, 1957) agrees that Congress "may have set itself up" for trouble by

larger context of Medicare subsidies they already received did little to assuage the anger of these high-income seniors. Most were probably unaware that these subsidies existed, while the minority who did comprehend the issue probably took these long-standing benefits for granted. Moreover, contrary to the beliefs of MCCA architects, the vast majority of elderly with incomes in the $30,000–$40,000 range simply did not consider themselves in any sense "wealthy" (see Tolchin 1989b).

Of course, arguments by supporters emphasizing the program's redistributive implications were intended to appeal not to the minority of affluent elderly liable for the surtax, but to the more than 60 percent of senior citizens who stood to receive considerable benefits at minimal personal cost. But such explanations and the furious response they provoked (mainly from high-income seniors) created added confusion among the majority of elderly "winners." Not aware of the subtleties of Medicare subsidies, they knew only that Congress had touted the MCCA as "a good deal" for the elderly and continued to defend the program while a group of fellow seniors angrily disputed these claims. The mere fact that so many disliked the legislation mitigated against the case made by supporters. If the MCCA was in fact beneficial for the elderly, why were so many writing their congressmen demanding its repeal?

Further, confusion among elderly winners only increased when a number of MCCA architects, apparently frustrated at their inability to increase support for the program, made remarks that appeared to criticize all senior citizens, not just those with the highest incomes, for MCCA's impending demise. "A lot of my colleagues are upset with the seniors," said Representative Stark in remarks aired on ABC News on September 18, 1989. "They say OK, the hell with them. If they are going to be this nasty, let's cancel the whole thing," he explained. "At some point, somebody has to abandon the notion that there's always someone else to pay for these things," agreed Senator Durenberger (Rovner 1989c, 1329).

Other statements that failed to distinguish between low-income and high-income seniors had to do with the implications of the elderly opposition to the MCCA for future policy-making. "If they can't take this one, what are we going to do when we get long-term care?" asked Senator Durenberger (Rich 1989d). Echoing this sentiment on NBC News on September 19, 1989, Representative Stark warned: "If the seniors think they are going to

---

telling the wealthy elderly "that they were getting a wonderful new benefit when, in fact, many of them could and did buy similar benefits privately at least as cheaply."

get nursing home care, which costs ten times more, without paying for a good share of it, they've got another guess coming" (see also Rovner 1988h, 3452).

By implying that all senior citizens were to blame for the MCCA's political troubles, program advocates undermined their own efforts to depict the legislation as highly beneficial to the 60 percent of the elderly with the lowest incomes. This group likely reasoned that if generalized elderly greed and selfishness were responsible for the unpopularity of the MCCA, maybe all senior citizens, even those with modest incomes such as themselves, were liable for the surtax. This, of course, was the mistaken belief that MCCA architects had labored so hard to counteract. Instead, such generalized attacks on the elderly called into question the motives of supporters and the veracity of their arguments on behalf of the program. They also unintentionally confirmed the misleading appeals of organizations like the National Committee.

Two additional phenomena undermined elderly support for the MCCA. The first concerned the program's design, which imposed premiums up-front (beginning in 1989) but phased in benefits gradually over a five-year period. Before passage, the legislation's architects had constructed the program in this manner for reasons of fiscal responsibility—if program costs exceeded estimates, financial reserves would cover the gap (see Chapter 3),[13] but once the MCCA became law this concept proved to be "a recipe for disaster" (Kosterlitz 1989c, 2454). While the affluent minority of elderly liable for the MCCA surtax protested immediately, the absence of many of the MCCA's most significant benefits left the low-income majority with little reason to support the program. Stated another way, the front-loaded design of the MCCA "ensured that the program had no chance to develop a wide constituency before it came under attack from those who didn't want to pay for it" (Weisberg 1989, 12). This political problem became more acute in April 1989, when the Congressional Budget Office projected a financial surplus in the program well in excess of previous estimates (see the discussion later in this chapter for further details).

During 1989, MCCA opponents sought to exploit these vulnerabilities by emphasizing the role the program's financial surplus would play in decreasing the federal deficit. MCCA's front-loaded design, they argued, essentially created a senior-financed "slush fund" (U.S. Congress 1989,

13. Social Security was structured in a similar manner when it was created in 1935.

S6184) to be used in deficit-reduction efforts.[14] "It adds insult to injury that seniors are not only being forced to pay for coverage that many already have but that their taxes will be used to cover up the true size of the deficit," charged National Committee President Martha McSteen (Rovner 1989b, 970). "The law we passed last year is socking it to the senior citizens and using that money to help meet Gramm-Rudman-Hollings targets," argued Senator Orrin Hatch (Rovner 1989c, 1401). "They're playing deficit politics with the pocketbooks of older people," agreed Representative Ron Wyden (Rovner 1989b, 970). Such criticisms took their toll on elderly support. Ironically, by the time of the repeal the program's front-loaded design would be seen not as a precedent-setting model for fiscally responsible policy-making, but as merely another attempt at obfuscation and deception by MCCA architects.

If the controversy surrounding the program's design surprised its advocates, the appearance of a separate though related source of displeasure—the continuing rise in Medigap premium prices—was even more unforeseen. During the original debate, program advocates had argued that the legislation's impact on well-to-do seniors would be mitigated by reductions in the cost of the Medigap policies that many would continue to purchase (at least until the program's benefits were fully phased in) (see Chapter 4). Contrary to these predictions, however, Medigap costs, fueled by increases in medical-care prices and utilization rates, continued to rise, even in the presence of the MCCA. In 1989, for example, one of the largest providers of Medigap policies—the Prudential Insurance Company (which sold coverage to 3 million AARP members)—would raise premiums by an average of 40 percent. Surprised by the level of cost increases like these, MCCA architects could only argue that such rates would have been 10 to 15 percent higher in the absence of the program (Tolchin 1989a). Unfortunately for the program's defenders, this point did not convince senior citizens, who had been promised that the legislation would actually reduce Medigap premiums, not just decrease the rate of such increases.

As opposition mounted during 1989, the MCCA architects struggled valiantly to come up with a politically acceptable means of reducing the program's supplemental premiums while preserving all or at least major

14. Unfortunately for defenders of the MCCA, the actions of the Bush administration during 1989 appeared only to confirm such accusations. Almost totally silent when it came to defending the importance of the legislation's benefits and the equity of its financing, administration interest in the legislation was motivated largely by its concern about the effect of repeal on the federal deficit. See the concluding section of this chapter for further discussion.

portions of its benefits. Each effort would meet with defeat, however, the vast majority undermined by constraints nearly identical to those present during the development of the legislation.

In April 1989 Senator Bentsen launched the first major attempt to save the MCCA when he announced that an unexpected surplus in program revenues had made it possible to reduce supplemental premium levels substantially. His proposal was based on recently completed reestimates of MCCA revenues and costs by the Congressional Budget Office and the Joint Committee on Taxation. Finding the elderly to be wealthier than previously estimated, the two bodies projected a program surplus of $9.1 billion over a five-year period—more than twice the amount legislated as actuarially necessary. "It was never our intention that beneficiaries pay more than needed to operate this program in a prudent and responsible fashion" (Rovner 1989a, 901), argued Bentsen, who immediately proposed reductions in the top supplemental premium from $800 to $500 in 1990 (by 1993, this cap would drop from $1,050 to $800).

The reaction from a number of MCCA supporters in Congress was positive, but Bentsen's plan drew strong opposition both from House Ways and Means Chair Rostenkowski and from President Bush. Not persuaded that the estimated revenues were excessive, Bush believed that the extra money would prove to be a necessity if, as the White House had insisted all along, the cost of the program's benefits, particularly prescription drugs, exceeded projections. "It would be imprudent to tinker with Medicare catastrophic insurance literally in its first few months of life" (Rovner 1989b, 969), argued the President in an April 21 letter to Rostenkowski. "Revenue-estimating is hardly an exact science," agreed the Ways and Means Chair in a statement urging fellow congressmen to support the President (Rovner 1989b, 969).[15]

Despite these objections, Bentsen's proposal might have prevailed if the conservative fiscal assumptions of Bush and Rostenkowski had proven unjustified. Unfortunately, however, events beginning in June 1989 only confirmed the latter's skepticism regarding the estimated surplus. In that month, new estimates from the Congressional Budget Office (CBO) indicated that the previously forecast $5 billion in excess revenue would be

15. Rostenkowski's displeasure with the Bentsen plan extended beyond concerns about its fiscal implications. In fact, his major objection appears to have been that Bentsen's actions effectively opened the door to those who wanted major revisions in the program or its outright repeal. "Once you open [the program] up, the fear is Bentsen can't hold it," said one aide to Rostenkowski (Kosterlitz 1989a, 1055).

consumed by the rising costs of the program's prescription-drug benefit (Rovner 1989f, 1782). Less than two months later the same body would inform Congress that the cost of the skilled nursing facility benefit, originally projected at $400 million yearly, could be as high as $2.4 billion a year based on the annual rate of increase since the new benefits started that January (Rovner 1989i, 2317; 1989j, 2398). Extrapolating from this figure, the CBO projected that the increasing cost of this benefit alone could add $10 billion to MCCA's cost over a five-year period. Fueled by the rising costs of prescription drugs and skilled nursing facility coverage, the CBO, at the end of August, projected the program's five-year cost at $45 billion, $15 billion more than expected at the legislation's passage and, equally as significant, $3 billion in excess of projected revenues (not only did no surplus exist, but the program was no longer self-financing!) (Rich 1989e). By October 1989, final CBO projections placed the five-year cost of the MCCA at $48 billion, 60 percent beyond original estimates (Tolchin 1989f).

As escalating benefit costs torpedoed Bentsen's surplus-reduction proposal, supporters turned their attention to other alternatives. A plan proposed by Representative Gradison and floated by Senator Bentsen sought to allow beneficiaries to opt out of the program if they also agreed to surrender coverage from the heavily subsidized Part B portion of Medicare. Although the measure's direct impact would be small (preliminary estimates indicated that 300,000 people, about one percent of all Medicare beneficiaries, would exercise this option), this was not its main purpose; instead it was intended as a symbolic device to focus beneficiaries on what "a good deal" Medicare, including the MCCA, really was (Rovner 1989h, 1959). The proposal was quickly rejected as opponents argued that tying catastrophic coverage to Part B amounted to little more than "blackmail" (Rovner 1989g, 1860) or "extortion" (Rovner 1989h, 1959) and, more important, would do little to mollify the angriest seniors, who would be subject to the surtax (most of whom were likely unaware that they received any subsidy from Medicare in the first place).

Other proposed reforms sought to broaden the MCCA financing beyond the elderly only. These included a proposal by Representative J. J. Pickle to make participation in the program truly voluntary (those opting out would retain full Medicare coverage) and compensate for the lost revenues by increasing the Medicare payroll tax from 1.45 percent to 1.60 percent (Rovner 1989g, 1859); a bill by Senator Carl Levin, Senator Tom Harkin, and Representative David Bonior to repeal the supplemental premium and

90	Catastrophic Politics

instead fund the program by raising the marginal tax rate on income in excess of $208,510 per couple ($109,050 for individuals) for all age-groups to 33 percent from 28 percent (Rich 1989b); and a plan by Stark that, among other things, also sought to eliminate the program's supplemental premium and make up part of the lost revenue by increasing the amount of wages subject to the Medicare payroll tax from $50,700 to $90,000 (Rovner 1989g, 1861). During the summer and fall of 1989 each was rejected, both because they broke the "fundamental premise of the program—that beneficiaries should pay for the new coverage"—and because members of Congress were loath to sponsor any measure that directly raised the taxes of working Americans (Rovner 1989g, 1859).

A major initiative from the House Ways and Means Committee sought yet another approach—namely, maintaining the program's elderly-only financing but structuring its costs in a more regressive manner (Rovner 1989h, 1957). The committee plan accomplished this by cutting the supplemental premium tax rate in half (from 15 percent to 7.5 percent) and making up the difference by substantially increasing the flat monthly premiums paid by all beneficiaries (from $59 to $109 annually in 1989). As a consequence, individuals with incomes between $15,000 and $45,000 (and couples between $25,000 and $80,000) would receive relief at the expense of individuals with incomes below $15,000 (couples, $25,000). Although uncomfortable with increasing costs imposed on the poorest elderly, the measure's proponents (Representatives Stark, Gradison, and Rostenkowski) reasoned that this alternative was the only remaining way to mollify many of the wealthiest elderly, who were complaining loudest about the supplemental premiums while preserving most of the program's benefits. (Although the proposal scaled back coverage for a number of items, including prescription drugs, it retained the basic structure of the benefits.)

However, in attempting to strike a new balance between the interests of the relatively affluent elderly and their low-income peers, the proposal pleased no one. It was summarily attacked and rejected both by program opponents (for failing to curtail the surtax completely) and by supporters (who complained that the proposal placed an unfair and severe burden on those who could least afford it) (Rovner 1989i, 2317).

As each proposal failed to muster the support of majorities in either the House or the Senate, and as calls for repeal mounted, MCCA architects abandoned their efforts to save all or most of the program's benefits. By October 1989 their final proposals, which significantly reduced both benefits and premiums, resembled the original Bowen plan more than the MCCA (Rovner 1989k, 2635–38). In the House an alternative authored by Representatives Stark, Gradison, and House Energy and Commerce Chair Henry Waxman repealed both the supplemental premium and the coverage for hospital stays, doctor bills, and skilled nursing facilities, retaining only a more-limited prescription-drug benefit, respite and home health-care coverage, and a few lesser items. Senate alternatives were twofold, including a relatively elaborate proposal by Senator Durenberger and a bare-bones approach offered by Senator John McCain. Durenberger's plan reduced the maximum surtax from $800 to $200 while repealing benefits for skilled nursing facilities and prescription drugs and raising the ceiling on doctor bills. By contrast, McCain's proposal retained only the program's flat premium to pay for coverage of hospital bills and home health and respite care, as well as a number of smaller benefits.

Had these bills been introduced in the winter or spring of 1989, they might have prevailed, but, by October the public mood regarding the MCCA had soured, and few in Congress were willing to go on record as supporting any action short of repeal. "We're just getting too much flak," said House Minority Leader Robert Michel, summing up this sentiment a month earlier (Rovner 1989j, 2397). "The only way to wash our hands, cleanse ourselves of the whole thing, is outright repeal." On October 4 the House did just that, rejecting the Stark-Gradison-Waxman proposal by a vote of 269 to 156 following a 360-to-66 vote to repeal virtually the entire program. Following its October 6 vote to reject Durenberger's proposal by a 62 to 37 vote, the Senate in a somewhat surprising move voted to approve McCain's plan by a vote of 99 to 0. However, the plan died one month later when House conferees refused to support even this skeletal proposal.

President Bush's acceptance of the repeal in November marked the extent of his administration's involvement with the legislation. Throughout 1989 the White House stood on the sidelines of the controversy, publicly opposing efforts to alter the program but unwilling to take any active role in saving it.[16] All things being equal, the Bush administration preferred that

16. The lone exception in the Bush administration was Secretary of Health and Human Services Louis Sullivan. On October 5, one day after the House vote to repeal, Sullivan sought to rally support for the legislation by strongly endorsing the Durenberger proposal. Only hours later, however, his endorsement was overruled by Office of Management and Budget Director Richard Darman, who stated that the President was taking no official position on any of the alternatives under consideration (Rovner 1989k, 2636). During November, Sullivan continued his efforts on behalf of the legislation, personally lobbying the White House to preserve as much of the program as possible. On this occasion he was also rebuffed as Bush

the legislation be preserved. Although it had little philosophical commit-ment to the program itself, the White House was concerned about the impact repeal would have on the federal budget deficit (Tolchin 1989d, 1989e). Because the MCCA's surplus had already been factored into federal budget estimates, eliminating the program would increase that year's deficit by several billion dollars, and in the process fail to meet the targets mandated under Gramm-Rudman-Hollings deficit-reduction legislation. The White House had little appetite for the politically painful task of compensating for the loss of such revenues with additional spending cuts or tax increases.

At the same time, however, the Bush administration was not inclined to bear any significant public criticism resulting from attempts to save the program. From the White House's perspective, the MCCA was the creature of a small and mostly Democratic group of congressmen who had a far greater stake in its preservation. Administration officials understood that the legislation's architects had considerable political capital invested in the program. They also knew that this group was still convinced that the program's benefits were significant and necessary to the well-being of elderly citizens. Calculating that the MCCA architects would, by political necessity, fight tenaciously to save the legislation, the White House was content to stand aside and let Congress take the political heat arising from any proposed reform.

During 1989 the Bush administration's refusal to become involved in efforts to save the MCCA proved immensely frustrating to the program's architects. Although it is unclear whether such intervention would have succeeded, supporters in Congress were undoubtedly disappointed, even bitter, at its absence. Summing up this sentiment following the defeat of his proposal to salvage some of the program's benefits, Senator Durenberger charged that the administration "was more interested in the politics of [the legislation] than the substance." If President Bush, he said, "had worked half as hard on catastrophic as he did on capital gains, there's no question in my mind we'd still have a catastrophic bill" (Rovner 1989k, 2636). "The message," concluded Durenberger, "is that you can't count on this White House to take a risk on health policy issues" (Greene 1989).

With the Bush administration refusing to intervene, Congress voted to repeal the MCCA just before the Thanksgiving recess in 1989. Following a

---

indicated his willingness to sign either a modified version of the McCain proposal or repeal (Rovner 1989m, 3239).

November 21 House vote to dismantle the legislation (passed by a margin of 352 to 63), the Senate at 1:52 A.M. the following day moved by unanimous consent to do the same. While the death of the program evoked both disappointment and bitterness among its supporters, program opponents viewed its demise with a mixture of vindication and relief. Whatever the reaction, though, one thing was apparent to all: the episode would not soon be forgotten. The implications and lessons stemming from the program's passage and repeal are the subject of the concluding chapter.

7

CONCLUSIONS

The Medicare Catastrophic Coverage Act of 1988, particularly in its method of financing, marked a major departure from previous policy-making in the area of social insurance. For the first time in the history of such programs, expanded benefits were to be funded entirely by those who were currently beneficiaries and would involve overt redistribution among them. In addition, the MCCA departed from the previously unstated but always abided-by principle that participation be worthwhile for all recipients—that is, that their benefits should exceed their costs.

Despite its revolutionary method of financing, the legislation won virtually unanimous support from those deeply involved in formulating it. For some, such as the American Association of Retired Persons, the decision to support the MCCA was largely pragmatic—a desire for the legislation's benefits, particularly prescription drugs and skilled nursing facilities, without saddling the low-income elderly with high costs.

For others, however, particularly the legislation's congressional architects, the interest was deeper—specifically, to establish a precedent for policy-making during an era of scarce resources. The legislation's more liberal architects saw the MCCA's method of financing as paving the way for future expansions of federal aid to the elderly, the most obvious being long-term care. Although few expected senior citizens alone to pay for the costs of such a program, any such effort would probably require significant contributions from this group, distributed in a progressive manner. By contrast, the more conservative architects foresaw similar financing principles being applied to deficit-reduction efforts or to related pursuits, such as preserving the long-run solvency of the Medicare A trust fund.

Unfortunately for supporters, the legislation's virtues, particularly those concerning financing, were largely lost on the elderly beneficiaries themselves. In the months following its passage, the program came under heavy attack, mainly from the relatively affluent minority who stood to pay premiums well in excess of the value of the program's benefits to them. At the same time, a confused majority of elderly due to receive the legislation's benefits at relatively minimal personal cost repeatedly failed to perceive the program as personally beneficial and consequently refused to rise to its defense.

As criticism from seniors mounted, the program's architects in Congress struggled to fashion a coherent and understandable case for the program, and particularly for its financing, but these efforts exacerbated rather than diminished the opposition. Unable to stem increasing criticism of the legislation, Congress voted in October and November 1989 to repeal outright virtually the entire program passed eighteen months earlier (with the important exception of spousal-impoverishment protection through Medicaid).

In the immediate aftermath of the repeal, the episode appeared to have two major effects on policy-making concerning the elderly. First, what originally appeared to be an emerging consensus in favor of a federal long-term-care program evaporated, largely because of disagreements over financing. This was illustrated by the 1989–90 deliberations of the Pepper Commission, a bipartisan committee of congressmen and congressional appointees charged with formulating a blueprint for long-term care (and health insurance for the uninsured). Members demonstrated considerable agreement on the benefits such a program would offer, but no financing proposal presented was acceptable to a majority (Pepper Commission 1990). It is interesting that in this case the concept of imposing significant costs on the elderly was scarcely considered; none of the financing proposals considered by the Pepper Commission called on the elderly to pay for more than a small fraction of the long-term-care program's estimated $43 billion yearly cost.

Second, Congress emerged from the episode with a renewed awareness of and heightened sensitivity to the perceived political power of the elderly. A cogent illustration of this phenomenon was seen in Congress's treatment of Medicare in the 1990 budget agreement. The original package agreed on by President Bush and congressional leaders in early October sought to increase monthly Medicare premiums from $28.60 to $54.30 between 1990 and 1995, as well as to double the yearly Part B deductible from $75 to

$150 during this period. Within days, however, senior-citizen advocacy groups and congressional supporters mobilized opposition to the plan and played a key role in defeating it (DeParle 1990; Pear 1990). The subsequent budget agreement, passed by Congress on October 27, included lower premiums ($45.60 a month by 1995) and Part B deductibles (increased to only $100). To offset the lost savings, Congress chose to redistribute the burden of the Medicare cuts by reducing reimbursements to physicians and by increasing the cap on the Medicare A portion of payroll taxes from $51,300 to $125,000 and indexing the cap in future years to increases in average earnings. The possibility of relating Part B premium increases to income was not even mentioned. Less than a year after the repeal, members of Congress had no stomach for any proposal that even resembled the MCCA's supplemental premium.

As the first two years of the Clinton presidency demonstrated, neither of these events portended the future of policy-making affecting the elderly. Whether or not elected officials desired to confront this set of issues, a number of serious problems, most involving difficult and politically unpleasant choices, remained to be addressed. The repeal of the MCCA once more left significant numbers of senior citizens liable for large portions of costs associated with extended acute hospital stays and physician services. Although most continued to purchase supplementary "Medigap" insurance to cover such expenses, the price of this insurance rose rapidly as health-care costs generally continued to spiral. In addition, the overwhelming majority of senior citizens continued to lack coverage for other major health-related expenses, including prescription drugs and, most significant, long-term care.

At the same time, elected officials, facing rising political pressure to reduce the federal deficit, were finding it increasingly difficult to overlook Social Security and Medicare, which in 1995 are projected to account for almost one-third of federal budget expenditures and more than 60 percent of entitlement spending (U.S. House, Committee on Ways and Means 1993, 1564, 1767). Also worrisome was the status of the Medicare A trust fund, projected in 1991 to become financially insolvent by the year 2005 in the absence of policy changes (U.S. House, Committee on Ways and Means 1992, 191–92). In light of such realities, lawmakers had little choice but to revisit a number of potentially controversial policy options that, like the MCCA, sought to curb the generous subsidies received by relatively affluent participants in Social Security and Medicare.

For those confronting such issues, the case of the MCCA presented a pair of cautionary lessons for policy-making in this environment. First, programs engaging in significant, overt income redistribution among large numbers of individuals may fail to garner broad public support when there is no deeply felt need for the program among beneficiaries or no widespread perception that some manner of crisis requiring public action exists. This study reveals that the MCCA, "an insider initiative driven by policy-analysis" (AARP 1989b), met neither of these conditions. Unlike the 1983 Greenspan reforms that Congress and the public reluctantly accepted as a last-ditch means of preserving Social Security's fiscal solvency, no comparable imperative existed for the degree of sacrifice the MCCA sought to impose on affluent beneficiaries. At the same time, the legislation failed to satisfactorily address long-term care, which was the preeminent health concern of the elderly. (Senior-citizen interest groups were keenly aware of this issue's potential. During this period they invested considerable political resources in their "Long Term Care '88" campaign, which sought to build support for a federally financed program among the public and elected officials.) The result was a program offering benefits that were not important enough to justify the relatively radical changes in its method of financing. In such an environment, the preferences of the intense minority who would be subject to the program's supplemental premium were easily able to overwhelm those of the marginally supportive, diffuse majority.

Four years after the MCCA's demise, as the nation prepared to debate President Clinton's health-care reform plan, politicians on all sides of the debate appeared to have learned this lesson well. Understanding that Americans will support nonincremental change in their health-care system only if they are persuaded that a health-care "crisis" actually exists, the major players in the debate spent considerable effort arguing the merits of this premise. Equally noteworthy was the Clinton administration's decision to finance its plan largely through indirect means—by taxing employers—instead of relying on such mechanisms as payroll taxes, where costs were more easily discernible. The administration undoubtedly believed that public objections to its program would be fewer if its redistributive effects were obscured.[1]

1. The administration's desire to downplay the redistributive effects of its plan became evident early in the health-care-reform battle in the aftermath of Health and Human Services Secretary Donna Shalala's admission that 40 percent of Americans who have health insurance would pay more for benefits under the Clinton plan. Republican opponents immediately seized on the 40 percent figure, emphasizing that—administration assurances to the contrary—many Americans would be significantly worse off under the plan (Clymer 1993). No doubt sensing the problems that would arise if health-care reform were to be perceived as a device for income

The second lesson of the MCCA, concerning the distribution of costs in social-insurance programs, has been a source of continuing debate among policy-makers. One perspective, offered mainly by officials of senior-citizen interest groups (including, most notably, AARP) and their supporters in Congress, holds that the episode demonstrates the political necessity of financing future programs more broadly—that is, in an intergenerational manner. According to this view, the fatal flaw of the legislation lay in its elderly-only method of financing. With low-income seniors deemed unable to shoulder more than a small fraction of the program's costs, such a mechanism essentially rendered its progressively distributed, highly unpopular surtax a fait accompli.

Adherents of this perspective argue that, among developed nations, the MCCA episode could have occurred only in the United States, because it alone fails to ensure that all citizens have essential health care, even while spending a significantly higher percentage of its GNP on health care than other nations. They emphasize this by comparing the U.S. health-care system with Canada's (Marmor 1993, 58). Both nations, they note, contain virtually identical proportions of elderly, report similar rates of medical-care use by the elderly, and experienced considerable economic stress in the 1970s and 1980s. Nevertheless, because Canada's medical-care program is universal, it has experienced virtually none of the controversy engendered by the growth of the elderly population in the United States. Indeed, references to "graying budgets," "greedy geezers," and "intergenerational equity" are unheard of north of the border.

Consequently, advocates of this first perspective argue that for future expansions of health-care benefits for the elderly (such as long-term care) to be viable politically, costs need to be dispersed throughout society, with the elderly shouldering no more than a small fraction of the burden (Kosterlitz 1989c, 2456). Following repeal of the MCCA, age-based organizations set out to achieve this objective by lobbying for improved health-care coverage for the elderly only as part of a larger effort to establish a national health insurance program for all Americans.

---

redistribution from rich to poor, the administration quickly sent Office of Management and Budget Director Leon Panetta off to Congress in an attempt to defuse the issue. Panetta, while contending that 70 percent of Americans would actually pay the same or less for health care under the Clinton plan, spent most of his testimony portraying the plan as an unmitigated benefit for all Americans. "If we fail to pass this plan," he said, "100 percent of Americans can be expected to pay higher insurance premiums because that is where costs are going right now" (Clymer 1993).

As early as 1990, AARP's National Legislative Council "called for a comprehensive national [health insurance] program that would assure care for young and old alike. . . . The council also recommended that AARP's board of directors support, promote, and assume a leadership role for a national health care program including long-term care" (*AARP Bulletin* 1990). By early 1993, the organization was by its own accounts "press[ing] the Clinton administration to include family long-term care services as a 'core component' in its still evolving health care reform program" (*AARP Bulletin* 1993).

While the Clinton health-care plan failed to provide benefits for long-term nursing-home care, it did respond to the demands of AARP and other age-based groups by including a prescription-drug benefit comparable to the one contained in the MCCA and by increasing coverage for long-term home care for severely disabled individuals (White House Domestic Policy Council 1993).

AARP's reaction to the proposal was complex. While describing the Clinton plan as "the strongest and most realistic blueprint to date for achieving our goals," the organization refused to endorse it specifically, despite a concerted campaign by the administration (Pear 1994a). Beyond concerns about proposed cuts in Medicare and Medicaid to help finance the President's program, AARP officials worried that the organization's members were confused about what was in the plan. "As people learn about the proposals, they are apprehensive and nervous," said one AARP leader, drawing an implicit parallel to the MCCA.

Nevertheless, AARP remained at the forefront of efforts to ensure comprehensive health care for all, including the elderly, through its role in the formation of the Health Care Reform Project. Comprised of more than thirty national groups, including Families U.S.A., the National Council of Senior Citizens, and the AFL-CIO, the coalition undertook a comprehensive public-education effort aimed at persuading Americans both that "an indisputable crisis" existed in the nation's health-care system and that only comprehensive reform would alleviate it (Health Care Reform Project 1994).

In contrast, with the perspective articulated by senior-citizen interest groups and their supporters in Congress, a second perspective, held mainly by a number of fiscally conservative public officials and policy experts, argues that the case of the MCCA points up the need to address issues concerning the financing of social-insurance programs in a clear and candid manner. More than a half-century after the creation of Social Security, and almost two decades following the establishment of Medicare, few among the elderly—and the public generally—have more than a dim awareness of the significant subsidies received by current beneficiaries through the two programs. As Chapter 1 makes clear, this phenomenon is not the product of historic accident; the efforts of program advocates to blur or hide the degree of redistribution occurring in Social Security and Medicare (both between and within cohorts of recipients) have served to preserve their significant antipoverty purposes.

According to adherents of this second perspective the MCCA demonstrated the impossibility of continuing this practice in the current resource-poor political environment. They argue that, for the foreseeable future, policy-making surrounding social-insurance programs will and/or should, by political necessity, be concerned with redistributing their resources in a more progressive manner, rather than imposing additional costs on younger generations. If these efforts are to be successful, the issue of the major subsidies received by the elderly through Social Security and Medicare, particularly those garnered by the most affluent, must be confronted explicitly and in a public manner. This task is undeniably a daunting one. Because for more than half a century the elderly have been encouraged to believe that all participants "earn" their benefits through contributions to these programs, extensive efforts over a significant period of time will probably be required to alter such perceptions.

Nevertheless, those adhering to this perspective believe that elected officials can no longer avoid this issue. To cite perhaps the most prominent example, the sheer size of Social Security and Medicare and the rising cost of the two programs, particularly the latter, virtually mandate that they will figure significantly in any effort to reduce the deficit. Proposals that fail to address the subsidy issue in a forthright and comprehensible manner might well follow the course of the MCCA, with the well-to-do elderly bitterly protesting that they have been unfairly singled out to pay a disproportionate share of their costs, while those with lower incomes fail to grasp the more positive (or at least less negative) implications of such reforms for them personally.

At the same time, the public's increased anxiety about the federal deficit has perhaps brought about a new willingness to consider reforms in Social Security and Medicare. As a result, proposals favoring increased income-targeting of benefits in such programs, if placed in the larger context of shared sacrifice among all Americans, may no longer spell likely political doom for politicians backing such plans.

This was clearly demonstrated in the case of the 1993 deficit-reduction plan proposed by Clinton and approved in modified form by Congress. The package of tax increases and spending cuts Clinton submitted to Congress included a proposal to increase from 50 percent to 85 percent the tax rate on Social Security benefits for high-income beneficiaries. Initial reactions to this aspect of the plan were predictably negative, as senior-citizen groups and their allies in Congress vowed to fight any attempt to reduce Social Security benefits to any segment of the elderly population (Toner 1993). However, this aspect of Clinton's larger program was accepted by Congress with little controversy as senior-citizen interest groups mounted only token opposition. Pragmatism, not altruism, was undoubtedly behind the senior-citizen lobby's tacit acceptance of what amounted to a reduction in Social Security benefits for the most affluent elderly. Such groups hoped Clinton would reward them the following year when the administration took up the issue of health-care reform. Nevertheless, advocates of entitlement reform would argue that the inclusion of a Social Security tax increase in the budget plan of a Democratic president and its acceptance by a Democratic Congress demonstrates that social-insurance programs have grown too large to be considered sacrosanct in future deficit-reduction efforts.

As Medicare's costs have continued to grow despite numerous efforts to restrain them, it is not surprising that the program remains a central target of efforts to trim federal expenditures and raise revenues. Indeed, a recent report by the Congressional Budget Office (1994) includes, as policy options for reducing the deficit, proposals to index and increase Medicare B deductibles; to increase co-insurance rates to 20 percent for home health services, laboratory tests, and skilled nursing facilities; to increase Medicare B premiums to cover 30 percent of program costs (from the current 25 percent rate); and, most significantly, to relate Medicare (as well as Social Security) benefits and costs to beneficiaries' incomes (so-called "affluence testing").

Thus far, support for such ideas, particularly the last, has come mainly from self-described "deficit hawks," such as former Nixon Commerce Secretary Peter Peterson (1993) and the newly formed Concord Coalition, a bipartisan group led by former Senators Paul Tsongas and Warren Rudman committed "to balancing the [federal] budget and keeping it balanced" (Concord Coalition 1994, 3). These proposals, however, could also be finding a following among more traditionally moderate-to-liberal sources—for example, the Urban Institute's Marilyn Moon (1993)—who see them as necessary to ensure Medicare's future solvency and pay for the program's expansion to include such items as long-term care.

Indeed, it is significant that among current elected officials one of the staunchest advocates of entitlement reform is Senator Robert Kerrey, a moderate Democrat from Nebraska who in 1993 was appointed by President Clinton to chair the thirty-two-member Bipartisan Commission on Entitlement and Tax Reform. Kerrey's recommendations, which included ending Medicare for wealthy senior citizens and reducing Medicare subsidies for the rest (Welch 1994), were harshly criticized by some commission members and failed to win support from the body as a whole (Pear 1994). Nevertheless, the fact that a politician like Kerrey, who is viewed as a potentially serious contender for the Presidency someday, would advocate such nonincremental measures could portend a further decline in the political sacrosanctity of Social Security and Medicare.

At present, it is unclear whether advocates for the elderly or those favoring entitlement reform will triumph fully or reach an accommodation in the foreseeable future. Nevertheless, the case of the MCCA is significant for having highlighted and clarified the policy issues they raise. Although the program proved to be a spectacular political disaster, the episode appears likely to provide public officials and experts with an improved understanding of the constraints inherent in social-insurance policy-making in the current political environment. As a consequence, the case of the MCCA may ultimately prove to be merely a failed first effort to confront this set of particularly complex and thorny policy issues.

Appendix ———————————————————

Multivariate Analyses
of AARP Survey Data

This Appendix presents the multivariate analyses briefly summarized in Chapter 5 in detail.

December 1988 Analysis

The first equation includes seven types or categories of variables hypothesized to affect opinion toward the MCCA. First, an income variable was included to measure the concept of self-interest, narrowly defined (several other variables also touch on the same concept). Given the program's progressive financing, we would expect income to influence opposition to the legislation.

Second, familiarity variables for each of the three income groups of elderly provide measures of the degree to which respondents believed they were familiar with the program (and ostensibly understood it). Given the progressive financing of the MCCA, we would expect the influence of self-rated familiarity to vary depending on one's income level. Specifically, familiarity is predicted to influence high-income elderly to oppose the program, low-income elderly to support it, and moderate-income elderly to fall somewhere between.

A third category of variables examines the extent to which beliefs and attitudes about specific benefits and costs—for example, the program's hospital coverage—affected opinions of the MCCA. Implicit here is the assumption that such attitudes were based on perceptions of the effect of such items on one personally. Of particular interest here is the variable relating to attitudes toward the supplemental premium. Given the central role ascribed to the premium in opposition to the MCCA by elected officials and the media, we would expect hostility to the premium to display a strong independent effect on opposition to the program.

Fourth, two variables measure assessments of the effect of program benefits and costs on the elderly in general. Inclusion of these items provides a gauge of opinion toward the program that is less directly related to narrow assessments of self-interest. For the two variables, positive assessments of the MCCA's utility for senior citizens are hypothesized to increase support for the program.

Fifth, two variables concerning the perceived effects of the MCCA's overall costs and benefits on one personally provide further measures of the effect of self-interest. Specifically, believing program costs outweigh benefits and that one is not likely ever to receive benefits under the program are predicted to influence opposition to the program.

Sixth, the duplicative-coverage variable measures the degree to which possessing such coverage (or believing one did) influenced opinion of the MCCA. Given that for those holding such policies the MCCA imposed additional costs while providing little or no additional coverage, possessing such coverage is hypothesized to increase opposition to the program.

Finally, the analysis includes two demographic variables measuring age and education, and two others measuring partisanship. The coefficients derived from the regression analysis are presented in Table A.1. In terms of coefficient size and statistical significance, two variables—assessments as to whether MCCA's costs justified its benefits for one personally, and attitudes concerning the supplemental premium—are found to provide highly influential explanations of opinions of the MCCA. Specifically, the belief that personal program costs were not worth benefits and antipathy toward the supplemental premium appear to be important factors responsible for opposition to the program. Related to these results, the duplicative coverage variable indicates that believing one possessed such coverage also proved influential in opposition to the program.

A number of other variables were found to affect opinions, particularly the two items concerning perceptions of the effect of the MCCA on senior citizens generally. Believing that the program was needed and would help older people in general influenced support for the program, while agreeing that program costs for older Americans were too high considering the benefits they received influenced opposition.

By contrast, variables measuring income and self-rated familiarity prove relatively unimportant in decisions to support or oppose the MCCA. Only the variable measuring familiarity among high-income elderly has a significant influence on the dependent variable, and then only at the .10 level.[1]

---

1. The findings with respect to income are somewhat surprising. The direction of the

Table A.1.   Multivariate analysis of variables on opposition to the MCCA, persons 65 +, December 1988

Variable	B	SE
Constant	3.928[a]	.7925
Income	− 8E-06	5E-06
Familiarity–High income	.1207[b]	.0703
Familiarity–Moderate income	.0506	.0601
Familiarity–Low income	−.0796	.0605
Likes hospital coverage	−.1116[c]	.0479
Likes outpatient coverage	.0028	.0435
Likes Rx coverage	−.0962[c]	.0399
Likes spousal-impoverishment provisions	−.1177[c]	.0504
Likes does not add to deficit	−.0133	.0377
Likes elderly paying all costs	.0638[b]	.0347
Likes $4 monthly premium	.0522	.0459
Dislikes supplemental premium	.1749[a]	.0380
MCCA should cover long-term care	−.0677[b]	.0354
Government should not be involved	.0020	.0329
MCCA is needed–all elderly	−.1591[a]	.0480
Cost high considering benefits–all elderly	.1046[a]	.0347
Cost worth it to you considering benefits	−.3904[a]	.0628
Expect to receive benefits	−.1305[c]	.0600
Possesses duplicative coverage	.1388[a]	.0532
Education	.0149	.0457
Age	.0051	.0085
Democrat	−.1056	.1463
Republican	−.0357	.1501

SOURCE: AARP Hamilton, Frederick & Schneiders Survey, December 1988; see appendix for exact question wording and coding of variables.

NOTE: N = 494, R square = .434.

[a]Significant at the $p < .01$ level.
[b]Significant at the $p < .10$ level.
[c]Significant at the $p < .05$ level.

February–March 1989 Analysis

While containing many of the same or similar items included in the December 1988 analysis, the equations derived from the February–March

income coefficient, significant at just above the .10 level, implies that increasing income increases *support for the MCCA*, exactly the opposite of what one would predict given the program's progressive financing mechanism. One possible explanation for this anomaly might be that other variables concerning assessments of program costs effectively account for the hostile attitudes one might expect wealthier elderly to have about the program. Thus, the effect of income alone is increased support for the MCCA.

1989 survey offer an opportunity to test the effect of knowledge on opinion of the MCCA. As discussed previously, this survey included fourteen true-false questions concerning specific aspects of the program. In Equation 1 of Table A.2, knowledge has been divided into two components: knowledge

Table A.2. Multivariate analysis of variables on opposition to the MCCA, persons 65 +, February–March 1989

	Equation 1		Equation 2	
Item	B	SE	B	SE
Constant	3.749[a]	.7103	4.109[a]	.6999
Income	-3E-06	5E-06	4E-06	5E-06
Familiarity–High income	.1437	.1130	.1067	.1018
Familiarity–Moderate income	.1236	.0995	.0757	.0896
Familiarity–Low income	−.1036	.0770	.0326	.0757
Supp. Prem.–High income	.8410[a]	.2297	.8868[a]	2332
Supp. Prem.–Moderate income	.7201[a]	.1963	.7958[a]	.2030
Supp. Prem.–Low income	.4435[a]	.1677	.4529[a]	.1696
Knowledge–High income	−.0507	.0354		
Knowledge–Moderate income	−.0316	.0316		
Knowledge–Low income	.0548[c]	.0248		
Beliefs–High income			−.1261[a]	.0540
Beliefs–Moderate income			−.0936[c]	.0437
Beliefs–Low income			−.0627[b]	.0381
How much one owes	9E-04[a]	3E-04	9E-04[a]	3E-04
How much one owes—Control	−.0145	.1235	−.0551	.1240
Believes receive benefits	−.3147[a]	.0530	−.2949[a]	.0534
Believes receive benefits—Control	−.7909[a]	.1789	−.7555[a]	.1796
How many benefit	−.1305[a]	.0362	−.1236[a]	.0364
How many benefit—Control	−.3701[a]	.1763	−.4313[c]	.1778
Duplicative coverage	.2762[c]	.1239	.2997[c]	.1236
Education	−.0025	.0504	−.0157	.0503
Age	−.0038	.0088	−.0045	.0089
Democrat	.0652	.1313	.0595	.1314
Republican	.0931	.1341	.0969	.1339
R square	.171		.173	

SOURCE: AARP EXCEL Poll 1, February–March 1989. See appendix for exact question wording and coding of variables.

NOTE: N = 762.

[a]Significant at the p < .01 level.
[b]Significant at the p < .10 level.
[c]Significant at the p < .05 level.

of the supplemental premium, and knowledge of the other aspects of the legislation. The supplemental-premium item is examined separately because, following passage of the MCCA, it was by far the most controversial provision believed to be contained in the program. Consequently, understanding this aspect of the MCCA independently may have been influential in decisions to support or oppose the program. Because one would expect knowledge to affect respondents differently, depending on their income level, the variables pertaining to the supplemental premium and other aspects of the legislation were split into three variables each, to reflect effects for high, moderate, and low-income groups of elderly.

Also included in the multivariate analysis were a number of variables concerning perceptions of how much one would owe under the legislation, how many would receive benefits, and the probability of personally receiving benefits. While different from variables on the December 1988 survey concerning perceptions of how program benefits and costs would affect one personally, these items constitute reasonable substitute measures of the influence of perceived self-interest on opinions. Other variables in the two equations reflecting income, self-rated familiarity, possession of duplicative coverage, and a number of demographic items are virtually identical to those included in the previous analysis.

The results of Equation 1 reveal that, in terms of directionality and significance, a number of key variables generally mirror the results of the previous analysis. First, income, familiarity, and the demographic and partisanship variables indicate no significant independent effect on opinion. Second, as in the December 1988 survey, items relating to perceptions of program costs (how much one owes, believes one receives benefits, and how many benefit) prove highly influential in such assessments. Also, believing that one possessed duplicative coverage was also influential in increasing opposition to the MCCA.

Regarding the variables measuring knowledge, general knowledge of the MCCA fails to affect opinion of the program for moderate and high-income groups while surprisingly influencing low-income elderly to *oppose* the program. At the same time, knowledge of the supplemental premium is found to increase opposition to the MCCA among all three groups, including (again counter-intuitively) the low-income elderly. For the high- and moderate-income elderly such results are plausible, implying that, for such persons, an understanding of who would pay the supplemental premium (those who pay more than $150 in federal taxes yearly)—not knowledge of other aspects of the legislation—was highly influential in decisions to oppose the program. In light of the high levels of hostility to the supplemental premium discussed earlier, such results make intuitive sense.

By contrast, interpretations of the effects of knowledge among the low-income elderly are far more problematic. Considering the fact that the program offered such persons significant benefits at little cost, and that virtually none in this group would be liable for any supplemental premium, it is surprising that knowledge (both general to the program and specific to the supplemental premium) appears to increase opposition to the program, rather than support.

How can one explain these anomalies? One possibility for these counter-intuitive results (and also for the failure of general knowledge variables to influence opinion among high- and moderate-income elderly) may be that the variables ostensibly measuring knowledge of the MCCA instead measure personal beliefs about the program. Stated another way, responses to knowledge items may have reflected respondents' perceptions of what they believed the program would accomplish, rather than factual understanding of such aspects. For example, in the case of the supplemental premium variable a correct answer to this item might have constituted an expression of displeasure with the surtax rather than evidence of knowledge. In other words, any question mentioning this term may have influenced respondents to choose the most hostile of the available responses—in this case, agreement with the statement that all who pay more than $150 in federal income taxes would pay the supplemental premium.

Similarly, responses to items encompassed within the variable measuring knowledge of other aspects of the MCCA may also be more reflective of beliefs than of knowledge. In order to test this proposition, the three variables measuring knowledge of the MCCA (the difference between correct and incorrect answers) were replaced by variables representing the extent to which one held positive beliefs about the MCCA. To create such a variable, the responses to twelve of the true-false items in the February–March 1989 survey were recoded as "1" if such an answer was likely to increase respondent support and as "0" if otherwise. For nine of the twelve items, positive perceptions were identical to factually correct answers. On the remaining three items, responses categorized as positive perceptions diverged from those that were factually correct. These items were recorded. Thus, for example, in the case of the item reading "[Under MCCA] Medicare will cover unskilled or custodial care in nursing homes if it is needed when you leave a hospital" a "true" answer (though incorrect) was recoded as "1," other answers as "0."

The results of the respecified analysis are set forth in Equation 2 of Table

A.2. Within each of the three income groups, holding positive perceptions increased support for the program.[2] Furthermore, the variables measuring knowledge of the supplemental premium by income group, reinterpreted here to signify negative perceptions of the provision, remain influential in decisions to oppose the MCCA. All other variables retain their directionality and significance.

In short, the respecified equation appears to result in a more readily interpretable model than the first, particularly with respect to the low-income elderly. Whereas the first model implied that possessing more knowledge (about the MCCA generally, and about the supplemental premium) caused this group to behave contrary to their self-interest (that is, to oppose the program), the second reaches a more plausible conclusion—namely, that perceptions concerning what the low-income elderly believed about the MCCA influenced their opinions of the program in a way that was consistent with their financial self-interest.

Survey Questions and Coding of Variables: Hamilton, Frederick & Schneiders Survey, December 1988, and EXCEL Poll 1, February–March 1989

Both Surveys

Opposition to / Support for the MCCA

Earlier this year, the federal government enacted a new "catastrophic care" health-insurance program. It is designed to protect older persons from the high costs of such things as long hospital stays, extensive prescription-drug use, and high out-of-pocket doctor's fees. This extra coverage is paid for in two ways: higher Part B Medicare premiums, and a supplemental premium based on the amount of tax a Medicare recipient owes.

2. The results of the three beliefs variables are highly sensitive to how they are specified. For example, if the variable is redefined as the difference between positive and negative perceptions of the program, the measures for high- and moderate-income elderly groups cease to be statistically significant. At the same time, the sign of the low-income coefficient changes and this variable is significant at the $p < .10$ level.

Do you support or oppose this "catastrophic care" program I just described to you? (IF CHOICE) Do you strongly or only somewhat [support/ oppose] this program?

Coding for multivariate analysis: 1 = Strongly support, 2 = somewhat support, 3 = no opinion, 4 = somewhat opposed, 5 = strongly opposed.

Income: Categories for Interaction Variables

Income was coded into three categories based on the likelihood of paying the supplemental premium: low-income elderly (singles with incomes below $10,000, couples below $20,000; moderate-income elderly (singles with incomes between $10,000 and $20,000, couples between $20,000 and $30,000); high-income elderly (singles $20,000 and above, couples $30,000 and above). For discussion of income categories, see Chapter 5, footnote 2.

Familiarity

How familiar are you with this new program—very familiar, somewhat familiar, not too familiar, not at all familiar?

Coding for multivariate analysis: 1 = not at all familiar, 2 = not too familiar, 3 = somewhat familiar, 4 = very familiar. Responses combined with income categories listed above.

Duplicate Coverage

Does this catastrophic-care coverage duplicate any private insurance coverage you now have?

Coding for multivariate analysis: 1 = no, 2 = don't know, 3 = yes.

Education

And what was the highest grade you completed in school? (IF IN GRADUATE SCHOOL, RECORD COLLEGE GRAD.)

Coding for multivariate analysis: 1 = 0–11, 2 = 12 (high school), 3 = 12+ (business school or some college), 4 = college graduate, 5 = graduate degree.

Age

For multivariate analysis, age is a continuous variable.

Party

Political party was coded into three categories: Democrat, Republican, and Independent. Respondents who leaned toward one party or another were coded into these parties, not as Independents. Coding for multivariate analysis: Democrat: 1 = Democrat, 0 = Republicans, Independents; Republican: 1 = Republican, 0 = Democrats, Independents.

HFS Survey

Income

On the survey itself, income was coded in the following manner: 1 = under $10,000, 2 = $10,000–$20,000, 3 = $20,000–$30,000, 4 = $30,000–$40,000, 5 = $40,000–$50,000, 6 = Over $50,000. For the multivariate analysis, median income levels were approximated for each category in the following manner: $7,000 = 1, $15,000 = 2, $25,000 = 3, $35,000 = 4, $45,000 = 5, $70,000 = 6.

Hospital Coverage

Except for an initial deductible of $540, the program covers the cost of very long hospital stays.

Coding for multivariate analysis: 1 = very negative, 2 = somewhat negative, 3 = don't know / no opinion, 4 = somewhat positive, 5 = very positive.

Outpatient Coverage

When it is completely phased in, the program will limit how much Medicare recipients pay for covered non-hospital (outpatient) medical services to about $1,400 a year.

For coding for multivariate analysis, see coding for hospital coverage.

Rx Coverage

When it is completely phased in, it will pay part *of the cost of prescription drugs after you have paid $600 a year.*

For coding for multivariate analysis, see coding for hospital coverage.

Spousal-Impoverishment Provisions

It helps protect the spouse of a Medicaid nursing home patient from losing everything to pay for care.

For coding for multivariate analysis, see coding for hospital coverage.

Federal Deficit

The program does not add to the federal deficit.

For coding for multivariate analysis, see coding for hospital coverage.

Elderly Pay All Costs of the MCCA

Medicare enrollees—those people who are eligible to receive benefits—will pay for the entire cost of the program.

For coding for multivariate analysis, see coding for hospital coverage.

$4 Monthly Premium

All Medicare enrollees will pay a $4-a-month basic premium for cata-strophic coverage.

For coding for multivariate analysis, see coding for hospital coverage.

Supplemental Premium

Everyone eligible for Medicare who pays more than $150 in federal taxes will pay (a separate, supplemental) an extra premium based on the amount of tax they owe.

Coding for multivariate analysis: 1 = very positive, 2 = somewhat positive, 3 = don't know / no opinion, 4 = somewhat negative, 5 = strongly negative.

Long-Term Care

The program does not go far enough in providing long-term nursing home and home health care benefits.

Coding for multivariate analysis: 1 = strongly disagree, 2 = somewhat disagree, 3 = don't know / no opinion, 4 = somewhat agree, 5 = strongly agree.

Federal Government Involvement

The federal government should not be involved in such an insurance program. They should leave it to private industry.

For coding for multivariate analysis, see coding for long-term care.

MCCA Is Needed—All Elderly

The program is needed and will be of help to older people in general.

For coding for multivariate analysis, see coding for long-term care.

Costs High Considering Benefits—All Elderly

The cost of the program to older Americans is too high considering the benefits they receive.

For coding for multivariate analysis, see coding for long-term coverage.

Costs Is High to You Considering Benefits

Do you think that the cost you will have to pay for the new catastrophic care coverage under Medicare is worth it to you considering the benefits?

Coding for multivariate analysis: 1 = no, 2 = don't know, 3 = yes.

Expect to Receive Benefits

Do you ever expect that you will receive the benefits from this new catastrophic care package under Medicare?

Coding for multivariate analysis: 1 = no, 2 = don't know, 3 = yes.

EXCEL Poll 1 Survey

Income

On the survey itself, income was coded in the following manner: 1 = less than $10,000, 2 = $10,000 but less than $15,000, 3 = $15,000 but less than $20,000, 4 = $20,000 but less than $25,000, 5 = $25,000 but less than $30,000, 6 = $30,000 but less than $40,000, 7 = $40,000 but less than $50,000, 8 = $50,000 but less than $75,000, 9 = $75,000 and over. For the multivariate analysis, median income levels were approximated for each category in the following manner: $7,000 = 1, $12,500 = 2, $17,500 = 3, $22,500 = 4, $27,500 = 5, $35,000 = 6, $45,000 = 7, $62,500 = 8, $80,000 = 9.

Supplemental Premium

Everyone eligible for Medicare who pays more than $150 in taxes will pay a supplemental premium based on the amount of tax they owe.

Coding for multivariate analysis: Equation 1: 1 = factually correct answer (true) constitutes knowledge of supplemental premium; 0 = incorrect response (false) or don't know represents an absence of factual knowledge of the premium; Equation 2: 1 = "true" response (although factually correct is reinterpreted to signify a negative perception of premium, in this case the belief that most or all elderly would be required to pay it), 0 = "false" or "don't know" response (reinterpreted here to represent a perception which is not negative).

Knowledge

For each respondent, coded as the difference between correct and incorrect answers to the thirteen true-false questions listed below. A factor of 7 was added to each respondent's score to create a positive scale.

Beliefs

For this variable, twelve of the thirteen true-false questions were recoded to represent the effect that holding a positive belief about some aspect of the MCCA would have on the dependent variable. (The item pertaining to the monthly premium was excluded because neither a true nor a false answer could be interpreted to reflect a positive belief.) Thus, for each respondent, the beliefs variable represents the sum of positive beliefs about specific aspects of the MCCA.

Hospital Coverage

Except for an annual deductible, Medicare now pays for all covered hospital costs as long as you need care.

Coding for multivariate analysis: Equation 1: 1 = correct answer (true), −1 = incorrect answer (false); Equation 2: 1 = "true" response (represents a positive belief about this aspect of the MCCA), 0 = "false" or "don't know" response (represents a perception about this aspect of the MCCA that is not positive).

Doctor Bills

Under Medicare Part B—the part that helps pay doctor bills—there is a maximum amount you or your health insurance have to pay each year in deductibles and co-payments.

For coding for multivariate analyses, see coding for hospital coverage.

Spousal-Impoverishment Provisions

The new law helps protect the husband or wife of a Medicaid nursing-home patient from losing all their income and assets to pay for care.

For coding for multivariate analyses, see coding for hospital coverage.

Mammography Screening

Medicare will cover mammography screening.

For coding for multivariate analyses, see coding for hospital coverage.

Hospital Deductibles

Every time you enter a hospital, you pay a deductible—so if you have three separate hospital stays a year—you pay three deductibles.

Coding for multivariate analysis: Equation 1: 1 = correct answer (false), −1 = incorrect answer (true); Equation 2: 1 = "false" response (represents a positive belief about this aspect of the MCCA), 0 = "true" or "don't know" response represents a perception about this aspect of the MCCA that is not positive.

AIDS

AIDS patients are automatically eligible for Medicare catastrophic coverage.

For coding for multivariate analysis, see coding for hospital deductibles.

Drugs

Although Medicare will begin to pay for prescription drugs used in a hospital or nursing home, it will not cover outpatient prescriptions.

For coding for multivariate analyses, see coding for hospital deductibles.

Maximum Premium

There is no upper limit to the Medicare premium computed on the basis of income tax that an individual will have to pay.

For coding for multivariate analysis, see coding for hospital deductibles.

Maximum Premium 2

A couple with $30,000 in annual income will have to pay the maximum supplemental premium.

For coding for multivariate analyses, see coding for hospital deductibles.

Physician Costs—Balance Billing

Medicare now limits the amount you pay each year for balance billing—in other words, even if your doctor charges more than the amount Medicare has approved, there is a maximum limit on what you will owe each year under Medicare Part B.

Coding for multivariate analysis: Equation 1: $1 = $ correct answer (false), $-1 = $ incorrect answer (true); Equation 2: $1 = $ true response (though factually incorrect) represents positive belief about this aspect of the MCCA, $0 = $ factually correct response (false) or don't know represents a perception about this aspect of the MCCA that is not positive.

Long-Term Care

Medicare will cover unskilled or custodial care in nursing homes if it is needed when you leave a hospital.

For coding for multivariate analyses, see coding for physician costs—balance billing.

MCCA Financing

Medicare enrollees will pay for part of the program through new premiums and working people will pay for the rest through a higher payroll tax.

For coding for multivariate analyses, see coding for physician costs—balance billing.

Monthly Premium

All Medicare enrollees will pay a new $4 a month basic premium for the catastrophic care coverage.

Coding for multivariate analysis: Equation 1: $1 = $ correct answer (true), $-1 = $ incorrect answer (false).

How Much One Owes

How much do you think you as an individual (or you and your spouse) will owe this year in additional Medicare premiums—both basic and supplemental—for the new catastrophic care coverage?

For multivariate analysis, How Much One Owes is a continuous variable. The control variable is coded as follows: 1 = respondents answering don't know or refusing to answer (coded 0 in first variable), 0 = all respondents giving estimates.

Believes Will Receive Benefits

Would you say that you or someone in your immediate family are very likely, somewhat likely, not too likely or not at all likely to ever personally receive benefits from this new catastrophic care program?

For multivariate analysis, "believes one will receive benefits" is coded as follows: 1 = not at all likely, 2 = not too likely, 3 = somewhat likely, 4 = very likely. The control variable is coded as follows: 1 = respondents answering don't know or refusing to answer (coded 0 in first variable), 0 = all respondents giving estimates.

How Many Will Benefit

About how many Medicare enrollees do you think will benefit each year from the new catastrophic coverage once all its benefits are in place?

For multivariate analysis, "how many will benefit" is coded as follows: 1 = less than 1 in 100, 2 = about 1 in 100, 3 = about 1 in 20, 4 = about 1 in 10, 5 = about 1 in 4, 6 = about 1 in 3, 7 = more than 1 in 3. The control variable is coded as follows: 1 = respondents answering don't know or refusing to answer (coded 0 in first variable), 0 = all respondents giving estimates.

Bibliography _____

American Association of Retired Persons (AARP). 1989a. "Millions of Americans need Catastrophic Health Care. And a better way to fund it." Advertisement. *Washington Post*, September 1, A9.
——. 1989b. "The Twelve Deadly Sins of Catastrophic." Unsigned internal memo. November 10.
AARP Bulletin. 1987a. "Congress Moves on 'Catastrophic' Bill as Support for Reform Effort Grows." June.
——. 1987b. "Bill Providing 'Catastrophic' Care Advances." July–August.
——. 1987c. "Battle Shapes Up over 'Catastrophic' Measure." September.
——. 1987d. " 'Catastrophic' Bill Nears Final OK as Senate Approves." December.
——. 1988. "How a Modest Idea Evolved into a Watershed Bill." February.
——. 1990. "A Fairer System: AARP Council Seeks National Health Plan." February.
——. 1993. "Clinton Told Care 'A Must.' " February.
AARP Research and Data Resources Department. 1989. *Opinions of Americans Age 45 and Over on the Medicare Catastrophic Coverage Act*. January.
AARP Vote. 1987. "Update on Catastrophic Care Legislation." Memorandum. April 14.
Arnold, R. Douglas. 1990. *The Logic of Congressional Action*. New Haven, Conn.: Yale University Press.
Bacon, Kenneth H. 1989. "New Initiatives for Health Care Are Endangered Following Drive to Defeat Catastrophic Care Act." *Wall Street Journal*, October 4.
Beilenson, Anthony C. 1988. "Neglecting What the Elderly Need Most." *Washington Post*, June 7.
Bernstein, Merton C., and Joan Brodshaug Bernstein. 1989. *Social Security: The System That Works*. New York: Basic Books.
Binstock, Robert H. 1983. "The Aged as Scapegoat." *Gerontologist* 23:136–43.
——. 1987. "The Implications of Population Aging for American Politics." Paper presented at the annual meeting of the American Political Science Association, Chicago.
Birnbaum, Jeffrey H., and Joe Davidson. 1988. "Medicare Expansion to Cover 'Catastrophic' Ills Viewed by Many Elderly as a Disaster Itself." *Wall Street Journal*, December 13.
Bluestein, Paul. 1988. " 'Catastrophic' Measure to Raise Taxes for Elderly." *Washington Post*, July 1.
Califano, Joseph A. 1988. "Health-Care Chaos." *New York Times Magazine*, March 20.

122   Bibliography

Clymer, Adam. 1993. "White House Tries New Numbers to Bolster Health Plan's Appeal." *New York Times*, November 5.

Cohen, Marc A., Eileen J. Tell, and Stanley S. Wallack. 1986. "The Lifetime Risks and Costs of Nursing Home Use Among the Elderly." *Medical Care* 24, no. 12, December, 1161–72.

Concord Coalition. 1994. *The Zero Deficit Plan: A Plan for Eliminating the Budget Deficit by the Year 2000*. Washington, D.C.

Congressional Budget Office. 1988a. *Trends in Family Income, 1970–1986*. Washington, D.C.: Government Printing Office.

———. 1988b. "The Medicare Catastrophic Care Act: Staff Working Paper." October.

———. 1988c. "Impact of the Medicare Catastrophic Coverage Act on Enrollees with Employment-Based Insurance Coverage." Memorandum. December 12.

———. 1989. *Subsidies Under Medicare and the Potential for Disenrollment Under a Voluntary Catastrophic Program*. Washington, D.C.: Congressional Budget Office, September.

———. 1994. *Reducing the Deficit: Spending and Revenue Options*. Washington, D.C.: Government Printing Office, March.

Cook, Fay Lomax, and Edith J. Barrett. 1992. *Support for the American Welfare State*. New York: Columbia University Press.

Davidson, Joe. 1988. "Older People's Lobby Gets a Message Across to All the Candidates." *Wall Street Journal*, March 8.

Day, Christine L. 1990. *What Older Americans Think: Interest Groups and Aging Policy*. Princeton, N.J.: Princeton University Press.

———. 1993. "Older Americans' Attitudes Toward the Medicare Catastrophic Coverage Act of 1988." *Journal of Politics* 55, no. 1, February, 167–77.

DeParle, Jason. 1990. "Furor on Medicare Cuts Offers Political Lesson." *New York Times*, October 12.

Derthick, Martha. 1979a. *Policymaking in Social Security*. Washington, D.C.: The Brookings Institution.

———. 1979b. "How Easy Votes on Social Security Came to an End." *Public Interest* 54:94–105.

Diegmueller, Karen. 1989. "Senior Citizens Revolt Against Catastrophic Aid." *Washington Times*, July 13.

Englund, Robert S. 1988. "The Catastrophic Health Care Blunder." *American Spectator*, November.

Fan, David P., and Lois Norem. 1992. "The Media and the Fate of the Medicare Catastrophic Extension Act." *Journal of Health Politics, Policy and Law* 17, no. 1, Spring, 39–70.

Ferrara, Peter J. 1988. "AARP: America's Biggest Tax Lobby." *Wall Street Journal*, April 28.

General Accounting Office. 1986. *Medigap Insurance: Law Has Increased Protection Against Substandard and Overpriced Policies*. GAO/HRD-87-8, October 17.

Gradison, Bill. 1989. "Still a Good Deal for the Elderly." *Cincinnati Enquirer*, February 3.

Greene, Marilyn. 1989. "Bush Sidesteps Catastrophic Care Issue." *USA Today*, October 11.

Health Care Reform Project. 1994. "The Factual Case for Reform." Undated press release.

Hewlett, Sylvia Ann. 1991. *When the Bough Breaks: The Cost of Neglecting Our Children*. New York: Basic Books.

Hosenball, Mark. 1989. "Letters Sealed with Fear." *Washington Post*, October 22.

Houston, Paul. 1989. "Catastrophic Care: It's Now Just a Catastrophe." *Los Angeles Times*, September 24.

Iglehart, John K. 1989. "Medicare's New Benefits: 'Catastrophic' Health Insurance." *New England Journal of Medicine* 320(5):329–35.

Iyengar, Shanto, and David R. Kinder. 1987. *News That Matters*. Chicago: University of Chicago Press.

Jacobs, Bruce. 1986a. "The Elderly: How Do They Fare?" Presented at the Working Seminar on the Family and American Welfare Policy, American Enterprise Institute, Washington, D.C.

———. 1986b. "The National Potential for Home Equity Conversion." *The Gerontologist* 26, no. 5, 496–504.

———. 1990. "Aging and Politics." In *Handbook of Aging and Social Sciences*, 3rd ed., ed. Robert H. Binstock and Linda K. George. New York: Academic Press.

Kingdon, John. 1984. *Agendas, Alternatives, and Public Policy*. Boston: Little, Brown.

Kingson, Eric R., Barbara A. Hirshorn, and Linda K. Harootyan. 1986. *The Common Stake: The Interdependence of Generations*. Cabin John, Md.: Seven Locks Press.

Kosterlitz, Julie. 1988 "Catastrophic Coverage a Catastrophe?" *National Journal*, April 29, 2949, 2952.

———. 1989a. "What Is Sen. Bentsen Up To?" *National Journal*, April 29, 1055.

———. 1989b. "Gray Power." *National Journal*, July 29, 1957.

———. 1989c. "Fiscal Catastrophe." *National Journal*, October 7, 2453–56.

Lambro, Donald. 1987. "Midwifery of a Catastrophic Plan." *Wall Street Journal*, February 10.

Light, Paul. 1985. *Artful Work: The Politics of Social Security Reform*. New York: Random House.

Linsky, Martin. 1986. *Impact: How the Press Affects Federal Policymaking*. New York: W. W. Norton.

Longman, Phillip. 1987. *Born to Pay: The New Politics of Aging in America*. Boston: Houghton Mifflin.

———. 1989. "Catastrophic Follies." *New Republic*, August 21.

Lowi, Theodore J. 1964. "American Business, Public Policy, Case Studies, and Political Theory." *World Politics* 16:677–715.

Margolis, Michael, and Gary A. Mauser, eds. 1989. *Manipulating Public Opinion: Essays on Public Opinion as a Dependent Variable*. Pacific Grove, Calif.: Brooks/Cole.

Marmor, Theodore R. 1973. *The Politics of Medicare*. 2nd ed. Chicago: Aldine Press.

———. 1988. "Coping with a Creeping Crisis: Medicare at Twenty." In *Social Security: Beyond the Rhetoric of Crisis*, ed. Theodore R. Marmor and Jerry L. Mashaw. Princeton, N.J.: Princeton University Press.

———. 1993. "Coalition or Collision? Medicare and Health Reform." *American Prospect*, Winter 1993, 53–59.

Marmor, Theodore R., Jerry L. Mashaw, and Philip L. Harvey. 1990. *America's Misunderstood Welfare State*. New York: Basic Books.

McCall, Nelda, Thomas Rice, and Judith Sangl. 1986. "Consumer Knowledge of Medicare and Supplemental Health Insurance Benefits." *Health Services Research* 20(6): 633–57.

Moon, Marilyn. 1993. *Medicare Now and in the Future.* Washington, D.C.: Urban Institute Press.

National Committee to Preserve Social Security and Medicare. 1987. "House Passes Flawed Catastrophic Care Bill." *Saving Social Security,* August.

———. 1988a. "Catastrophic Health Care Update: Legislative Conference Planned." *Saving Social Security,* March.

———. 1988b. "A Message to Congress: Seniors Won't Thank You." Advertisement. *Washington Post,* March 31.

———. 1989a. "Ambitious Catastrophic Fix Unveiled." *Saving Social Security,* May.

———. 1989b. Letter to Representative Dan Rostenkowski. June 27.

———. 1989c. Untitled press release. July 18.

———. 1989d. "Catastrophic Care Debate Reopened." *Saving Social Security,* September.

———. 1989e. Untitled press release. September 7.

———. 1989f. Letter to Representative Dan Rostenkowski. October 30.

Newsweek. 1989. "The Elderly Duke It Out." September 11, 42–43.

New York Times. 1987a. "Text of Statements by Reagan and White House." February 13.

———. 1987b. "Reagan Threatens a Medicare Veto." July 22.

———. 1988. "Freedom from Health Fear." July 2.

———. 1989. "The New Medicare: No Catastrophe." January 27.

Niemi, Richard G. 1983. "The Future of Public Opinion Research Theory and Methods." Paper delivered at the annual meeting of the American Political Science Association, Chicago, September.

Page, Benjamin, and Robert Y. Shapiro. 1992. *The Rational Public: Fifty Years of Trends in Americans' Policy Preferences.* Chicago: University of Chicago Press.

Page, Benjamin I., Robert Y. Shapiro, and Glenn R. Dempsey. 1987. "What Moves Public Opinion." *American Political Science Review* 81:42–43.

Pear, Robert. 1987a. "Reagan Proposes Health Insurance for Major Illness." *New York Times,* February 13.

———. 1987b. "Congress Seeks a Fair Way to Pay for Catastrophic Health Insurance." *New York Times,* June 7.

———. 1987c. "Reagan Assails House Bill to Cover Major Illness Cost." *New York Times,* July 26.

———. 1987d. "Medicare Expansion: The Debate over Spending." *New York Times,* October 28.

———. 1990. "Cost Increases for Medicare Recipients Stir Protests." *New York Times,* October 2.

———. 1994a. "Clinton Fails to Get Endorsement of Elderly Group on Health Plan." *New York Times,* February 25.

———. 1994b. "Panel on U.S. Benefits Overhaul Fails to Agree on Proposals." *New York Times,* December 15.

Pepper Commission, U.S. Bipartisan Commission on Comprehensive Health Care. 1990. *A Call for Action.* Washington, D.C.: Government Printing Office.

Peterson, Mark A. 1993. "Institutional Change and the Health Politics of the 1990s." *American Behavioral Scientist* 36, no. 6, 782–801.

Peterson, Peter G. 1993. *Facing Up: How to Rescue the Economy from the Crushing Debt and Restore the American Dream.* New York: Simon & Schuster.
Peterson, Peter G., and Neil Howe. 1988. *On Borrowed Time: How the Growth in Entitlement Spending Threatens America's Future.* San Francisco: ICS Press.
Pollack, Ronald F. 1987. "For Many, the Health Plan Is Catastrophic." *New York Times,* March 25.
Pratt, Henry J. 1976. *The Gray Lobby.* Chicago: University of Chicago Press.
Preston, S. H. 1984. "Children and the Elderly: Divergent Paths for America's Independence." *Demography* 21:435–37.
Prokesch, Steven. 1987. "Medicare Expansion Under Fire." *New York Times,* February 12.
Rasky, Susan F. 1989. "Stage Set for Congressional Battle with Elderly on Tax for Medicare." *New York Times,* January 12.
Rice, Thomas, Katherine Desmond, and Jon Gabel. 1989. *HIAA Research Bulletin: Older Americans and Their Health Coverage.* October.
Rich, Spencer. 1987a. " 'Catastrophic' Plan Advances in the House." *Washington Post,* June 18.
———. 1987b. " 'Catastrophic' Bill's Costs Raise New Doubts," *Washington Post,* September 14.
———. 1987c. "Health Bill Passage Predicted." *Washington Post,* September 23.
———. 1987d. " 'Catastrophic' Care: A Look at Innovations." *Washington Post,* November 2.
———. 1989a. "Catastrophic Insurance Attacked as Unfair Tax." *Washington Post,* January 15.
———. 1989b. "Cut Debated in Premium for 'Catastrophic' Plan." *Washington Post,* June 2.
———. 1989c. "Bentsen Favors Cutting New Premium." *Washington Post,* June 25.
———. 1989d. "Medicare Coalition Shaken by Its Own Handiwork." *Washington Post,* July 27.
———. 1989e. " 'Catastrophic' Cost Estimate Rises Sharply." *Washington Post,* August 24.
Ripley, Randall B., and Grace A. Franklin. 1984. *Congress, the Bureaucracy, and Public Policy.* Homewood, Ill.: Dorsey Press.
Rovner, Julie. 1987a. "Reagan Sides with Bowen on Medicare Plan." *Congressional Quarterly,* February 14, 297.
———. 1987b. "Panel Considers Alternatives to Bowen Plan." *Congressional Quarterly,* March 7, 434.
———. 1987c. "House Panel Approves Catastrophic Care Plan." *Congressional Quarterly,* May 9, 915–18.
———. 1987d. "New Medicare Plan May Include Drug Coverage." *Congressional Quarterly,* May 23, 1082.
———. 1987e. "Senate Panel Approves Medicare Expansion." *Congressional Quarterly,* May 30, 1136–37.
———. 1987f. "Two Panels Add Drug Coverage to Medicare." *Congressional Quarterly,* June 20, 1327–28.
———. 1987g. "Pepper Leaves Mark on Catastrophic-Care Bill." *Congressional Quarterly,* July 18, 1591.
———. 1987h. "House OKs Medicare Expansion Despite Reservations over Cost." *Congressional Quarterly,* July 25, 1637–39.
———. 1987i. "Catastrophic-Costs Measure Back on Track Despite Delays." *Congressional Quarterly,* October 31, 2677–79.

——. 1987j. "Pepper Wins a Round on Long-Term Care Bill." *Congressional Quarterly*, November 21, 2874–75.

——. 1988a. "Catastrophic-Costs Conferees Irked by Lobbying Assaults." *Congressional Quarterly*, March 26, 777, 780.

——. 1988b. "Elderly Group Continues to Thrive . . . But Image on Capitol Hill Still Tarnished." *Congressional Quarterly*, March 26, 778–79.

——. 1988c. "Long Term Care '88: Campaign for an Issue." *Congressional Quarterly*, April 9, 939.

——. 1988d. "Dispute over Drug Benefit Slows Catastrophic-Costs Bill." *Congressional Quarterly*, May 14, 1290.

——. 1988e. "Pepper's Push Propels Health-Costs Bill." *Congressional Quarterly*, May 21, 1402.

——. 1988f. "Pepper Bill Pits Politics Against Process." *Congressional Quarterly*, June 4, 1491–93.

——. 1988g. "Singing His Praises, House Says 'No' to Pepper." *Congressional Quarterly*, June 11, 1605.

——. 1988h. "Catastrophic-Insurance Law: Costs vs. Benefits." *Congressional Quarterly*, December 3, 3450–52.

——. 1989a. "Surtax Reduction a Possibility, but Critics Demand Repeal." *Congressional Quarterly*, April 22, 901–2.

——. 1989b. "Bush, Rostenkowski Say 'No' to a Medicare Surtax Cut." *Congressional Quarterly*, April 29, 969–70.

——. 1989c. "Senate Finance Tilting Toward a Cut in Medicare Surtax." *Congressional Quarterly*, June 3, 1329–30.

——. 1989d. "Authors Defend Health-Costs Law." *Congressional Quarterly*, June 3, 1330.

——. 1989e. "Catastrophic-Coverage Law Narrowly Survives Test." *Congressional Quarterly*, June 10, 1400–1402.

——. 1989f. "Panel May Pave Way for Death of Catastrophic-Costs Law." *Congressional Quarterly*, July 15, 1781–83.

——. 1989g. "Catastrophic-Costs Dilemma Grips Ways and Means." *Congressional Quarterly*, July 22, 1859–61.

——. 1989h. "Catastrophic-Costs Proposal Pleases Almost No One." *Congressional Quarterly*, July 29, 1956–59.

——. 1989i. "Senate Tries Revision of Catastrophic Costs Law." *Congressional Quarterly*, September 9, 2316–17.

——. 1989j. "Finance Weighs Benefit Cuts in Catastrophic-Costs Law." *Congressional Quarterly*, September 16, 2397–98.

——. 1989k. "Both Chambers in Retreat on 1988 Medicare Law." *Congressional Quarterly*, October 7, 2635–38.

——. 1989l. "The Catastrophic-Costs Law: A Massive Miscalculation." *Congressional Quarterly*, October 14, 2712–15.

——. 1989m. "Catastrophic-Coverage Law Is Dismantled by Congress." *Congressional Quarterly*, November 25, 3238–39.

Shick, Allen. 1989. "Health Policy: Spending More and Protecting Less." In *The Care of Tomorrow's Elderly*, ed. Marion Ein Lewin and Sean Sullivan. Washington, D.C.: American Enterprise Institute.

Stanley, Harold W., and Richard G. Niemi. 1992. *Vital Statistics on American Politics*. 3rd ed. Washington, D.C.: Congressional Quarterly Press.

Straw, Margaret K. 1990. "Polling on the Medicare Catastrophic Coverage Act:

Findings and Lessons Learned." Paper presented at the Annual Conference of the American Association for Public Opinion Research, Lancaster, Pennsylvania.

Thompson, Carolyn Rinkus. 1990. "The Political Evolution of the Medicare Catastrophic Health Care Act of 1988." Ph.D. Dissertation, Johns Hopkins University.

Tierney, John. 1988. "Old Money, New Power." *New York Times Magazine*, October 23.

Tolchin, Martin. 1988. "New Health Insurance Plan Provokes Outcry over Costs." *New York Times*, November 2.

———. 1989a. "Recipients of Medicare Also Face Rise in Cost of Private Insurance." *New York Times*, February 12.

———. 1989b. "Retreating on Pledge, White House Hints at Tax Increase to Aid Elderly." *New York Times*, July 18.

———. 1989c. "Expansion of Medicare Is Painful for Congress." *New York Times*, September 13.

———. 1989d. "In Face of Protests, Bush Decides to Back Change in Medicare Plan." *New York Times*, August 27.

———. 1989e. "Medicare Repeal Mood and Catastrophic Illness." *New York Times*, September 19.

———. 1989f. "How the New Medicare Law Fell on Hard Times in a Hurry." *New York Times*, October 9.

Toner, Robin. 1989. "Back in Grass Roots, Congressman Is All Ears." *New York Times*, August 8.

———. 1993. "Clinton's Social Security Test: Selling Sacrifice to the Elderly." *New York Times*, February 7.

Torres-Gil, Fernando. 1989. "The Politics of Catastrophic and Long-Term Care Coverage." *Journal of Aging and Social Policy* 1(1/2):61–86.

U.S. Congress. 1987. *Congressional Record*. 100th Congress, July 22, H6461–545; October 13, S14090–105; October 23, S15021–23, S15086–183.

———. 1988. *Congressional Record*. 100th Congress, June 2, H3854–99; June 7, S7257–67, S7386–414.

———. 1989. *Congressional Record*. 101st Congress, June 6, S6164–87; June 7, S6293–323; October 4, H6566–616; October 6, S12824–907.

U.S. House of Representatives, Committee on Energy and Commerce, Subcommittee on Health and the Environment. 1987. *Medicare and Medicaid Catastrophic Protection*. Washington, D.C.: Government Printing Office, Serial 100-74.

U.S. House of Representatives, Committee on Ways and Means. 1990. *Background Material and Data on Programs Within the Jurisdiction of the Committee on Ways and Means*. Washington, D.C.: Government Printing Office, WMCP 101-29.

———. 1992. *Background Material and Data on Programs Within the Jurisdiction of the Committee on Ways and Means*. Washington, D.C.: Government Printing Office, WMCP 102-44.

———. 1993. *Background Material and Data on Programs Within the Jurisdiction of the Committee on Ways and Means*. Washington, D.C.: Government Printing Office, WMCP 103-18.

U.S. House of Representatives, Committee on Ways and Means, Subcommittee on Health. 1987. *Catastrophic Illness Expenses*. Washington, D.C.: Government Printing Office, Serial 100-7.

U.S. Senate, Committee on Finance. 1987. *Catastrophic Health Insurance*. Washington, D.C.: Government Printing Office, S. Hrg. 100-169, pts. 1-3.
———. 1990. *Catastrophic Care: Excess Revenues*. Washington, D.C.: Government Printing Office, S. Hrg. 101-519.
U.S. Senate, Committee on Finance, Subcommittee on Health. 1987. *Long-Term Health Care*. Washington, D.C.: Government Printing Office. S. Hrg. 100-35.
Vogel, Ronald J. 1988. "An Analysis of the Welfare Component and Intergenerational Transfers Under the Medicare Program." In *Lessons from the First Twenty Years of Medicare*, ed. Mark V. Pauly and William L. Kissick. Philadelphia: University of Pennsylvania.
Wall Street Journal. 1987. "Ducking Social Security." November 19.
———. 1988. "The AARP Tax." June 17.
———. 1989. "AARP's Catastrophe." October 2.
Washington Post. 1987. "The House Votes on Health." July 21.
———. 1988a. "A Good Health Bill." May 27.
———. 1988b. " 'Catastrophic' Handbook Set for Distribution." September 19.
———. 1988c. "Belling the Catastrophe." December 16.
———. 1989. "Maneuvering on Catastrophe Hill." September 22.
Weisberg, Jacob. 1989. "Cat Scam." *New Republic*, October 30, 11–12.
Welch, William M. 1994. "Benefit Cuts Proposal Under Fire." *USA Today*, December 12.
White House Domestic Policy Council. 1993. *The President's Health Security Plan*. New York: Times Books.
Wilson, James Q. 1992. *American Government: Institutions and Policies*. 5th ed. Lexington, Mass.: D. C. Heath.
Yankelovich, Daniel. 1991. *Coming to Public Judgement: Making Democracy Work in a Complex World*. Syracuse, N.Y.: Syracuse University Press.

Index ————————————————————————————————

Made in the USA
Lexington, KY
19 December 2013